D0129134

The Great Book of Chocolate

To Terrie -
Big chocolate
chocolate (with
kisses (with
raspberries *

THE GREAT BOOK OF
chocolate

The Chocolate Lover's Guide

WITH RECIPES

David Lebovitz

FOOD PHOTOGRAPHY BY
Christopher Hirsheimer

TEN SPEED PRESS
Berkeley | Toronto

Copyright © 2004 by David Lebovitz

All rights reserved. No part of this book may be reproduced in any form, except brief excerpts for purpose of review, without written permission of the publisher.

Ten Speed Press
Box 7123
Berkeley, California 94707
www. tenspeed.com

Distributed in Australia by Simon & Schuster Australia, in Canada by Ten Speed Press Canada, in New Zealand by Southern Publishers Group, in South Africa by Real Books, and in the United Kingdom and Europe by Airlift Book Company.

Cover and book design by Nancy Austin
Food photography by Christopher Hirsheimer
Prop styling by Peggi Jeung
Food styling and location photography by David Lebovitz:
    page 22, 28, 46, 53, 57, 62, 63, 64, 65, 67, 72
Location photography by Michael Lamotte: pages 12, 74, 76, 78, 81
Photos on page 14 reprinted courtesy of Scharffen Berger
    Chocolate Maker.
Photo on page 49 reprinted courtesy of Recchiuti Confections

Ten Speed Press thanks the following for their generosity in loaning and contributing props for the food photographs: Panetti's, Pomp Home, and Dandelion, all in San Francisco.

Library of Congress Cataloging-in-Publication Data on file with publisher.

Printed in Singapore

First printing, 2004

1 2 3 4 5 6 7 8 9 10 - 08 07 06 05 04

Contents

Acknowledgments

I'd like to thank the following chocolate makers and confectioners for generously teaching me, allowing me to nose around while they worked, and, when I got lucky, letting me sample the finest chocolates that I could have possibly imagined: Fran Bigelow of Fran's Chocolates (Seattle), the staff and chefs at Callebaut Chocolate (Weize, Belgium), Chantal Coady of Rococo (London), Jean-Jacques Bernachon of Bernachon (Lyon, France), Denise Acabo of A l'Etoile d'Or (Paris), Eric Case and Chocolates El Rey (Venezuela and United States), Marie-Anne Dufeu and the chef-instructors at École Lenôtre (Paris), Frederick Schilling and Tracey Holderman of Dagoba Organic Chocolate (United States), Gary Guittard of Guittard Chocolate (San Francisco), Thierry Lallet of Saunion (Bordeaux, France), Katrina Markoff of Vosges Haut Chocolat (Chicago and New York), the late Lionel Poilâne of Poilâne bakery (Paris), Yachana Jungle Chocolate (Ecuador and United States), Martine Pechenik of Martine's Chocolates (New York City), Michael Recchiuti of Recchiuti Confections (San Francisco), Richard Donnelly of Richard Donnelly Chocolates (Santa Cruz, California), John Scharffenberger and Robert Steinberg of Scharffen Berger Chocolate Maker (Berkeley, California), Steven Wallace of Omanhene chocolate (Ghana and United States), and Timothy Moley of Chocolove organic chocolate (United States).

Chocolate kisses to the talented bakers who contributed their favorite chocolate recipes: Flo Braker, Letty Flatt, Fran Gage, Michael Lewis-Anderson, Susan Herrmann Loomis, Nick Malgieri, Mäni Niall, Lee Posey, Patricia Rain, Kathleen Stewart, Carolyn Weil, and Joanne Weir.

Merci beaucoup to Paul and Myriam Wittamer from the Wittamer chocolate shop in Brussels, Belgium, and their incredibly sweet and hardworking staff, for allowing me a rare glimpse of their very special chocolate shop.

Tremendous thanks to photographer Christopher Hirsheimer, who brilliantly captured my desserts (and anything chocolate covered that I left in my wake) with stunning sophistication and simplicity. Thanks, too, to Peggi Jeung for infusing the book with a contemporary style, and to Nancy Austin for her beautiful vision and making sure everything fit perfectly on these pages.

Appreciation to Shari Saunders and Eric Haeberli for their assistance and good cheer during the photo sessions, and to Anne Block for helping me guide folks in pursuit of the best chocolates from around the world—and for managing to sample *just one more* hot chocolate with me along the way.

Much appreciation to editor Lorena Jones at Ten Speed Press, who handed me this wonderful project, allowed me great freedom, and let me loose to pursue my passion for chocolate (this is *work*?), and to Ten Speed editor Aaron Wehner, for providing support and for being just an all-around good guy.

And to my agent Fred Hill, for overcoming a regrettable excess-of-chocolate episode in his past to get behind this project.

Introduction

Every time I put a piece of chocolate in my mouth, the entire world grinds to a screeching, blinding halt. I can't seem to focus on anything else, except that first smooth rush—the incredible taste and sensation that only comes from chocolate.

Initially, there's the unmistakably sweet, slightly bitter sensation as I savor that first taste, allowing the chocolate to slowly dissolve in the warmth of my mouth. As the chocolate continues to melt, intense flavor overwhelms me, and my whole face relaxes, which happens whenever I eat something so perfect, signaling that I am truly content. The following sensations become a complex jumble of flavors as the chocolate takes control. As I begin to chew, an entirely new sensation, wonderfully exotic yet comfortable and familiar, takes over and I am, once again, seduced. That luscious, unbelievable, aromatic, roasted, complex, beguiling, and incomparable satisfaction that I get from chocolate is unmatched by anything else I could possible eat.

Chocolate. I cook it, taste it, bake it, melt it, coat things with it, burn it (occasionally), temper it, spread it, ice cakes with it, and make candy from it. Chocolate occupies my thoughts just about every day. Even as I write this, I'm nibbling on chocolate! Chocolate, in my biased opinion, is the most universally provoking and addictive flavor. As a professional pastry chef for years, I know the power that chocolate holds over people. If you don't have chocolate on your dessert menu in the restaurant business, you may as well head home.

The Great Book of Chocolate, is a gift to all chocolate lovers: a compact, yet comprehensive guide to the world of chocolate. Culinary trend watchers point to an exceptional, and stronger-than-ever, excitement about chocolate. And while teaching cooking classes and leading tours, I've found that the interest in chocolate increases as each year passes.

And now there are so many chocolates to choose from! Imported and domestic chocolates, artisan chocolates, mass-produced chocolates, single-bean chocolates, flavored tablets, bars of spiced organic chocolate, high cacao percentage chocolates (such as 99%, 72%, 64%, and more), "dark" milk chocolates, and chocolates filled with everything from crackly praline paste to soft, nutty nougat. New American brands, roasted and blended in small quantities using vintage equipment, are noteworthy for their richness and depth of flavor. The best Belgian chocolates are conched for days to achieve their incredible smoothness. And in France, small confectioners are roasting and grinding their own beans for enrobing chocolates to sell exclusively in their elegant boutiques. There's even a socially conscious company that dips crunchy organic cacao nibs in a sweet coating of pineapple juice and cane syrup (fabulous!). But has this new wave of chocolate making almost gone too far? One haughty French manufacturer of chocolate is not only naming their chocolates for the region that the cacao used comes from, but also labeling some with the date of cacao harvest.

I've learned quite a bit as I've written and tasted. Having never appreciated milk chocolate, working on this book has changed my perception dramatically. A bold Venezuelan milk chocolate flavored with malt, which gave an incredible depth to the sweet richness of the milk chocolate, converted me. In the past, I had often dismissed milk chocolate as very sweet and not very chocolaty, or as John Scharffenberger of Scharffen Berger Chocolate Maker in Berkeley says "chocolate used merely as a food coloring." I now happily use premium milk chocolate in my desserts, often when paired with another ingredient that needs to dominate, such as citrus or spicy flavors. I even learned about people dubbed "supertasters" (page 34), who have ultrasensitive taste buds and can detect more flavors, intensity, and bitterness in chocolate than most people.

Within this guide to the world of chocolate, you'll also find a concise history of cacao, spanning from warring ancient Aztec natives right up to the proud contemporary European and American manufacturers' use of the latest technology combined with principles from the distant past. I found a whole new breed of chocolate makers using chocolate to make a social statement, educating the public to the plight and pillage of tropical rain forests. You'll read how chocolate is made and discover the characteristics and nuances of dark chocolate, milk chocolate, white chocolate, and other products containing chocolate.

And as if anyone needs an excuse to eat chocolate, medical research has uncovered startling discoveries about the effects of chocolate on blood cholesterol levels. Is it truly a mood-enhancer and stress releaser? Some are even touting chocolate as a dental health enhancer and as an important and rich source of antioxidants, which are widely believed to ward off many diseases.

As I worked on this book, I straddled two continents: Europe and North America. I was fortunate to tour factories and take professional classes, working with excellent chefs in France, Belgium, and the United States.

I spent time at the Callebaut chocolate factory near Brussels, where raw cacao beans are shipped directly from the rain forests. Emptied from their burlap sacks, each bag is labeled with country of origin, the name of the exporter, and the weight. The dusky beans are sorted, roasted, pounded, and pummeled until a smooth mass is achieved. I watched in amazement as the warm dark, liquid mass was poured into molds and cooled to form shiny, tempting chocolate blocks. I was able to work with their chefs, creating towering and delicious works of art from the finest Belgian chocolate.

In London, the delightful and properly British shop Rococo, operated by Chantal Coady, offered me tastes of chocolates scented with flavors such as rose geranium, lavender, and Earl Grey tea (which would be quite delicious served alongside a pot of correctly brewed British tea).

I marveled at the chocolate makers and confectioners of France, particularly at Bernachon in Lyon and Sauinon in Bordeaux, creating edible works of art of incredible beauty and flavor. Each morsel of chocolate became an individual work of art. Smooth ganache-filled bonbons, suave bittersweet truffles, and dark, crispy, caramelized Florentines coated with swirls of chocolate became delicious research.

In the San Francisco Bay Area, I visited and roasted cacao beans at Scharffen Berger Chocolate Maker. They've been credited for transforming the entire image of high-end chocolate making in the United States, which was previously thought to be exclusively the domain of European chocolate makers and now has become an important addition to the American artisanal food movement. I toured Guittard Chocolate Company near San Francisco, one of the oldest chocolate makers in existence, long popular within the American chocolate industry and now with the public as well...and still family owned and operated. I was thrilled to taste their latest chocolates made from unusual cacao beans they've procured especially for crafting chocolates that feature these rare varietals of cacao.

I witnessed young chocolatiers who are pioneering fabulous and creative ways of working with chocolate to please a newly discerning and appreciative public. I loved sampling San Franciscan Michael Recchiuti's new-fashioned Whoopee Pies and S'mores, being seduced by the sexy spiced orbs of truffles at Vosges Haut Chocolat in Chicago, and I stood fascinated at the activity of Richard Donnelly in his laid-back shop just a few blocks from the waves of the Pacific Ocean, in the surfing community of Santa Cruz, California.

I also spent quite a bit of time learning about and tasting chocolates in shops abroad. In Paris, more so than anywhere else in the world, pâtisserie and confectioners are creating the most extraordinary desserts imaginable with chocolate. I was amazed at the creativity of Pierre Hermé, who continues to challenge the rules and has emerged as arguably the greatest pastry chef in the world. Robert Linxe has kept La Maison du Chocolat at the top of just about everyone's list of favorite chocolate shops by making his chocolates the essence of singular simplicity and luscious perfection. And the venerable Lenôtre boutiques are still going strong in Paris with a line of chocolates using beans of various African origins. I watched and learned and dipped with the chefs at the École Lenôtre, a school for professionals near Paris. We created fabulous chocolate decorations and candies, working magic with little more than a bowl of melted chocolate, a slab of marble, and a skilled hand.

The question I am most often asked is, "What's your favorite chocolate?" Instead of being concerned about what *I* like, I want you to learn what *you* like. Don't be persuaded by chefs, advertising and marketing campaigns, or magazine articles with tastings and ratings to tell you what is best. Each of us enjoys a different chocolate experience. You may like dark bittersweet chocolate with the heavily roasted flavor found in *forastero* cacao beans from Africa. Or perhaps you prefer the more delicate floral aroma of chocolate made with Venezuelan *criollo* beans. Others crave the sweetness and silky texture of milk chocolate, domestic or imported. And how about white chocolate? It seems that people either love it or could easily go without it. Just for the record, I love it. I find it provides an exceptional contrast in desserts and confections made with pure dark bittersweet chocolate.

The fun of chocolate is that there are so many new brands to consider and sample, all made from beans produced with unprecedented craftmanship. There are beans with unique origins, beans with qualities and nuances dependent on careful hand-harvesting methods, still-primitive cacao fermentation techniques that take place right within the tropical cacao-producing regions, and precise roasting and blending in modern factories. The new world of chocolate is constantly being remolded by chocolate makers striving to perfect their craft, motivated by an increasingly interested and educated public. We need to appreciate the work of these masters, with the knowledge that the creation of fine chocolate is a labor of love by all involved in its making, from the farmer who nurtures the raw beans of the fruity cacao pods to the chocolatier who fashions the polished slabs of well-crafted chocolate.

I made sure to include the recipes that showcase my passion for all things chocolate. This means riffs on classics such as rich, nutty brownies (pages 111 and 112), to indulgent wedges of pitch-black Chocolate Fitness Cake (page 100). And who can resist perfectly moist Black-Bottom Cupcakes (page 104)? These are the chocolate treats that I like to make and eat. I use few adornments and I keep it simple, preferring to keep the focus on the intensity of chocolate. To augment my collection of favorite recipes, I asked some wonderful bakers and professional chefs for their favorite, most delicious chocolate recipes and then adapted them for home cooks' use. Most recipes you'll be able to easily re-create in your home kitchen, using everyday ingredients and equipment. But if you have the slightest amount of ambition, make my recipe for Rocky Road (page 144). The only thing more satisfying than whipping up a batch of billowy homemade marshmallows is devouring the finished crunchy, nutty, and gooey confection.

My hope is that you'll use this book to understand chocolate, whether you like to bake with it, constantly snack on it, or just look forward to that gilded box signifying a special occasion. Throughout history, wars have been fought for chocolate, class struggles have been defined by chocolate consumption, and chocolate harvesting and trading have realigned nations and caused sociopolitical upheavals and reforms. And the taste, manufacturing, usage, and consumption of chocolate has reflected these events and come to reflect the human struggle with economic, environmental, and political realities. Let this knowledge increase your appreciation of chocolate *and* the rain forest.

Once you understand the beauty of the mysterious and exotic cacao plant, and learn the process that transforms the treasured cacao bean into the incredible confection that we know as chocolate, you can't help but become as passionate about all things chocolate as I am!

Chocolate Explained

Chocolate is a product of the fruit of the cacao tree. The fruits grow off the main trunk of the tree as pods, similar in size to a deflated football. The trees can grow anywhere from 25 to 50 feet tall. Once harvested, each pod is cut open to reveal a milky white or pastel-hued pulp, with loads of beans—20 to 50 per pod—embedded. Split apart, cacao pods have characteristics similar to a melon but with much larger seeds (cacao beans) and little flesh. The vast majority of cacao trees grow within rain forests where the climate is very warm and humid, roughly 20 degrees north and south of the equator.

During the first 2 to 3 years of their lives, the fragile cacao tree seedlings must be sheltered from the strong, direct sunshine of the tropics, hence the need to preserve the shade-bearing foliage of the rain forests for chocolate producers. Mature cacao trees that provide shade, thereby protecting the younger trees, are called "cacao mothers." Tropical food products, like chocolate and coffee grown under these conditions, are often labeled "shade-grown"—a designation given to foliage that is culti-vated under the canopy of the rain forest.

However, due to the deforestation of the rain forest, banana leaves often need to be layered over cacao seedlings to provide the necessary shady environment for the young and delicate plants. Although the cacao pods are tough, the trees themselves, both young and mature, are susceptible to many diseases and pests. Once the trees are mature and begin to bear fruit, when they are 5 to 8 years old, they can handle direct sunlight without difficulty and the trees become far more tolerant of less-than-ideal growing condi-tions and pest exposure, while also developing greater resistance to damage.

There are 3 main varieties of cacao, although due to natu-rally occurring cross-pollination and genetic mutation, many varieties share characteristics with other strains. This makes absolute positive identification difficult. Many seedlings, for example, are transported great distances by birds (in their droppings), reseeding other areas with different varieties of cacao. Other cross-pollinating is done by ants, midges, and aphids. And cross-hybridizing, done by humans to promote more vigorous and hardy cacao trees (see *trinitario*, page 11), has contributed to making definitive identification perplexing.

This can make the significance of chocolate labeled as "estate-grown" somewhat meaningless; unless a specific variety of bean is used in the chocolate and stated on the label, one estate can cultivate several different varieties of cacao. And even in cases where the chocolate label claims one particular variety of cacao bean, tastes vary due to the method of fermentation as well as subsequent roasting time and temperature.

FORESTERO

Forestero is by far the most common and prolific cacao, due to its hardiness and resistance to diseases and pests. Stout and tannic *forestero* beans are fermented for about a week to mellow them, a relatively long period of time. Grown primarily in Africa, *forestero* beans are the workhorses of the chocolate world. Africa accounts for about 70% of the world's production of cacao. Questionable working conditions on the Ivory Coast have caused some chocolate makers to become more conscientious when selecting the origin of their cacao.

Although many lesser-quality chocolates are made from *forestero* beans, skilled chocolate makers often blend *forestero* beans along with *trinitarios* and *criollos* to provide balance and give the chocolate a longer, more complex finish and depth.

CRIOLLO

Criollo beans are considered the highest grade and are used for top-quality chocolate blends and many single-bean chocolates. The elongated *criollo* pod is low yielding and vulnerable to disease, making the beans far more costly than *forestero* beans. There are few true *criollo* beans available due to their vulnerability. Many have been cross-pollinated or hybridized. The majority of fruity and aromatic *criollo* beans are harvested in Venezuela; the rest come from Indonesia and Madagascar. They are low in astringency and require less fermentation than harsher beans, about 3 days of fermentation as opposed to up to 7 days for *forestero* beans. *Criollo* beans account for only about 5% of the total world production of cacao.

The Best Cacao Bean in the World?

One of the most magnificent chocolates that I've encountered was made from a true *criollo* bean, Ocumare, from Chocovic (www.chocovic.es), in the Catalan region of Spain, outside Barcelona. The deep, dark bar of Ocumare chocolate was handed to me by Katrina Markoff of Vosges Haut-Chocolate (page 67) and contained approximately 71% Ocumare cacao. This extraordinary and exotic chocolate was sharp and direct at first bite— and fabulously intense. The flavor continued to develop while I let it dissolve in my mouth, first slightly acidic, then mellowing to lush and earthy. The difficult-to-harvest Ocumare bean is rare and expensive due to the low-yielding nature of the tree. It is a totally engrossing chocolate experience and just about every chocolate expert I know agrees that Ocumare is the most extraordinary cacao. An Ocumare chocolate is also created and distributed by El Rey (page 154).

TRINITARIO

Trinitario cacao is a hybrid of *forestero* and *criollo*, created on the island of Trinidad. *Trinitario* cacao was developed to be less resistant to disease than *criollo* beans, like *forestero* beans, but to possess many of the same fruity qualities as the sought-after *criollo*. The best *trinitario* beans are from Java and, of course, Trinidad.

You should not necessarily think that chocolate brands that promote the use of "only *criollo* beans" in their chocolate are necessarily better than others. Although *criollo* beans are often of high quality, I know several conscientious chocolate makers who blend various *trinitario* and *forestero* beans to achieve their particular flavor balance. I've tasted other excellent chocolate blends and have come to the conclusion that many of my favorite chocolates use a combination of several cacaos: *criollo* for its lovely floral notes and *forestero* for longer chocolate finish, or *trinitario* beans, which have the characteristics of both *criollo* and *forestero*, for a perfect balance of flavors.

HARVESTING, FERMENTING, AND SUN-DRYING

Harvesting of the cacao pods is quite difficult. Since the trees are too fragile to allow the workers to climb, the pods must be harvested at ground level. Because the pickers are down on the ground, they must be skilled in their judgment, using their expertise to peer up from far below to determine which cacao pods are just ripe for picking. Each pod is carefully removed from the trees using *tumnadores*, wielded by the skilled pickers who go through the forests and deftly slice the pods from the trees, being careful not to damage the fragile bark and harm the tree. *Tumadores* are special, machete-like "cacao blades" mounted on long handles.

Once the pods are harvested, they're sliced open, revealing light-colored beans surrounded by a creamy white, pastel pink, or soft violet–hued pulp. Natives make a drink from this pulp (you can sometimes find it in cans in Latin markets), or it is drained away during the fermentation process. The fermentation of the beans is the first, and considered by many to be the most important, part of the entire chocolate-making process that determines the final taste and flavor of the beans, and consequently, the finished chocolate. Fermentation takes place in pits dug in the earth or in wooden crates. Once heaped into the pits or crates, the cacao beans and their gluey

pulp are covered with banana leaves and left to ferment. Fermentation turns the sugars into acids and changes the color of the beans from a pale color to a rich, deep brown. To save money, some processors dry their beans over an open fire, which gives the cacao a charred, almost oily, resinous flavor that is hard to disguise and undesirable in premium chocolate.

Once fermented, the beans are sun-dried, although in particularly moist climates, the beans are sometimes dried using heaters to prevent mold growth. During the drying process, the beans lose most of their moisture. As the beans are laid out to dry, they are manually raked and turned daily to ensure even drying.

Sun-drying takes about a week, and the growers use this opportunity to pick through and remove any foreign matter from the beans. Once dried, the beans are packed into canvas or woven polypropylene sacks for shipping. Most beans are sold on the world commodities market, the prices varying depending on quality and supply and demand. Although most cacao beans are shipped abroad, in Ghana, Omanhene (page 68) dark milk chocolate is produced in the African community where the beans are grown. Similarly, El Rey chocolate (page 154) is made in Venezuela, where all of their beans are grown.

ROASTING AND PROCESSING

Once cacao beans arrive at factories, they are unloaded and sorted for foreign objects. (Sometimes shoes, knives, rocks, and other objects are found.) Then the cacao beans are carefully roasted to a temperature between 210°F and 290°F (100°C and 145°C). After they're roasted, they're expelled from the hot roaster and cooled quickly. Next they are passed through a winnower, which cracks the dusky outer shells from the beans and blows them away. The meaty, valuable inner bean is crushed into smaller pieces, known as "nibs," to be made into chocolate.

Cacao nibs are high in fat, about 50 percent. They're crushed into a paste, using granite stones or heavy-duty metal, a process that can take several hours or several days. During this time, the fatty nibs are continuously rolled and ground, generating heat and releasing the cocoa fat, which helps them liquefy until a smooth paste is formed. This paste is called "chocolate liquor," although it contains no alcohol. The process is called "conching." Unsweetened or bitter chocolate is referred to as pure chocolate liquor and is mostly sold in bars for baking. Unlike bittersweet or semisweet chocolate, no cocoa butter is added to unsweetened chocolate so it isn't very fluid when melted and should not be used in recipes when bittersweet or semisweet chocolate is called for.

In general, the longer the conching, the better the chocolate. As the cacao paste is kneaded smooth, cocoa butter and coarse sugar are blended in (the large sugar crystals help provide abrasion to smooth the rough cacao nibs) to make a chocolate that is called bittersweet or semisweet. Milk chocolate is made by kneading in dried milk solids or milk powder, in addition to the cacao butter and sugar, during the blending process.

The Essence of Chocolate

When cacao beans are ground into chocolate, the beans, which are quite fatty, become warmed up by the heat naturally produced by the pulverizing action of the rollers. Some of the "top notes" of flavor are lost during the heating and some manufacturers of chocolate products add chocolate extract to replace these important flavor components.

I discovered Star Kay White chocolate extract when I wrote my first cookbook and I was contacted by Ben and Jim Katzenstein, who, incidentally, had attended my college in upstate New York. Their small company was founded in 1890 by immigrant relatives. Star Kay White extract is made by steeping cacao beans in a base of alcohol in the same manner that pure vanilla extract is produced. I had never heard of chocolate extract, and I am naturally wary of any "flavoring enhancers" used by food processors. Yet when I twisted open the top of the amber bottle and sniffed apprehensively, I was surprised by the intense aroma of roasted cacao, a full expression of chocolate. I began experimenting, using their chocolate extract like vanilla extract, adding a generous teaspoon to many of my chocolate desserts. Now I find myself reaching for that bottle when making a batch of brownies, or to add to the batter of a rich chocolate cake. I have found that chocolate extract certainly does enhance the exquisite chocolate flavor of just about everything I make.

Their chocolate extract is available in 8-ounce bottles for home cooks at specialty stores and through their website, www.starkaywhite.com (1-800-874-8518).

LET THE CANDY MAKING BEGIN

Some companies ship the finished chocolate directly to large candy companies in liquid form, which saves both the chocolate company and the confectioner time, money, and resources.

If the manufacturer is to shape the chocolate into bars, blocks, chips, or *pistoles* (small disks, which are preferred by professional bakers because they're easy to measure and temper), the chocolate must be tempered (page 89). To temper chocolate, the temperature of the melted chocolate is lowered, then carefully raised to stabilize and emulsify the cocoa butter. Once the chocolate is perfectly tempered, it is immediately deposited into molds, which are vibrated to release any air bubbles. After a trip though an air tunnel or cooling chamber, the firm, shiny chocolate is released from the molds then wrapped and sealed for storage and shipping.

A BRIEF HISTORY OF CHOCOLATE

By analyzing ancient pottery, experts agree that the discovery of chocolate belongs to the Toltec tribe in Central America, as early as around 600 B.C. At first, only the milky pulp surrounding the beans within the pod, called *cupuaçu*, was used as a drink by the Toltecs. It's likely they found the raw seeds too unpleasant to enjoy. Eventually, however, the Toltecs learned to cook the beans by roasting them over a fire to make them somewhat palatable in their furtive quest for food sources. Once they discovered how tasty the roasted beans were, the now-precious cacao beans ascended in value to the point where they began to be traded as legal currency as well as a food source. A pumpkin could be had for 4 cacao beans, a rabbit for 10, and a slave for 100. Although the Toltecs became a prosperous group for many years, an eventual downward spiral of economic and social stagnation set the stage for their subsequent conquest by the Aztecs, who became transfixed by those dusky beans; they began pulverizing cacao into a drink by blending the bean sludge with water. To do this, they developed a tool called a *molinillo*, a wooden staff with decorated mixing rings, a blending tool still used today in just about every Latin American country.

During his conquest of Mexico in 1519, the Spanish explorer Cortés discovered that the Indians, both the working class and the nobles, were enjoying this odd drink called *xocolatl* (pronounced *chocolatl*). Although the nobility flavored the drink with sweeteners or chile, the common folk diluted the pricey bean paste with inexpensive cornmeal. The Spanish settlers began experimenting with cacao by augmenting it with nuts and pungent spices brought from their homeland. Of course, word (as well as the taste) of this new drink caused a huge sensation back home in Spain, which, at the time, was enjoying prosperity. Sipping chocolate became all the rage, a tasty impetus for the newly rich to show off their privilege and wealth, often enjoying and sharing sweetened chocolate as a drink at socials.

The popularity of chocolate soon spread from Spain throughout Europe, most notably into France (via the Basque regions of Bayonne and Biarritz), and Italy, where dainty ladies enjoyed it and transformed the enjoyment of chocolate into a highly refined social event. Many paintings from this period depict women leisurely reclining while enjoying a porcelain demitasse of steaming chocolate. Such ceremony is reflected by the beautiful porcelain, silver, and copper chocolate pots now sold by antique dealers or even displayed in museums. Symbolic of the social values of the era, these pots are distinct and unmistakable, with their carved wooden sticks inserted through a hole in the lid to blend the chocolate, reminiscent of

the great book of chocolate

Cacao or Cocoa?

Cacao refers to the pod (cacao pods), the beans within (cacao beans), and the pure paste of the bean (cacao paste or cacao "liquor").

Cocoa is the powder made from the cacao bean, which is mashed into a paste then pounded to extract the cocoa butter and pulverized into a dry powder. It is believed the name "cocoa" came about as the result of a mis-spelling by early English traders.

the *molinillos* used by earlier chocolate lovers. Chocolate pots are still sold and used, mostly in Europe.

By the seventeenth century, chocolate was indeed a sensation throughout Europe and cacao came to be cultivated and farmed in increasing amounts to keep up with the demand. The problem was that cacao beans still needed to be ground by hand the old-fashioned way, which was mostly done back in Mexico. The pounding and grinding was done with a metate, a slablike mortar and pestle, and strong-armed women worked the cacao into a paste, then compressed the fat-rich mass into cylinders or rounds. The laborious work required made chocolate expensive and exclusive, since not much could be produced at a time. (In many less-developed countries, cacao beans are still pounded with a metate into a paste and hand shaped into cylinders, then grated into a powder as needed, using a sharp kitchen grater.)

Eventually, in their quest to automate chocolate making, enterprising Europeans developed mechanical grinders and processing machines. Now the laborious task of crushing and grinding chocolate was replaced by machinery and heavy stone conchers, which rather effortlessly transformed the rough cacao mass into a smooth paste through the motion and heat of the stone rollers grinding away. Soon there was enough chocolate for just about everyone who wanted it, and it was no longer the exclusive beverage of the wealthy and powerful elite. And by the 1820s, cacao trees were introduced into Africa and South America.

The first full-scale, relatively modern chocolate factory was set up in Britain in 1728, followed by several more across Europe. In Holland, Coenraad Van Houten developed a method for separating the cacao mass from the cocoa butter, producing what we refer to as cocoa powder, and revolutionized the chocolate-making process. Human hands were still necessary, but much of the heavy-duty kneading was now done by machines. The Swiss are generally credited for shaping the first modern bar of chocolate in 1819, even though the Aztecs were known to make chocolate "bars" by spreading smooth cacao paste onto a banana leaf and drying it in the sun until it hardened. Another important development came out of the desire and eventual ability to knead dry milk paste into chocolate to enhance its nutritional properties. This became the first version of what we know as milk chocolate. Daniel Peter incorporated dry milk powder into chocolate in the mid-1870s. Rudolphe Lindt of Switzerland developed the first refined conching techniques, which made possible what we now think of as high-quality, smooth, silky chocolate.

Once the machinery was in place, chocolate production and distribution over the next few years quickly became democratized: *chocolate for everyone!* The more chocolate became available, the more it was consumed. And, as chocolate products and palates became more refined, the spices popular in earlier times were no longer added. The newest and possibly the greatest innovation of the twentieth century was made by a Belgian manufacturer in 1912. Jean Neuhaus developed techniques for making pralines, known elsewhere as dipped or filled chocolates, or bonbons. And just a few years later, across the Atlantic, the Milky Way bar was developed in the United States by the Mars corporation and then the famous Mars bar which revolutionized the American candy and chocolate business.

Sweet Success in Hershey, Pennsylvania

Today, Hershey's is still the biggest success in the world of chocolate. Hershey's is the most recognizable and widely known chocolate. In fact, the Hershey bar is the best-selling chocolate bar in the world. Milton Hershey began his success by founding a caramel company. It was wildly successful, and he eventually sold the entire caramel factory for the then unheard-of price of $1 million. Mr. Hershey, then built a factory in Hershey, Pennsylvania, which became the largest chocolate manufacturing plant in the world. In addition to the chocolate factory, the town of Hershey became a project of Mr. Hershey, as he built schools, housing, and recreational facilities, as well as provided services to his employees. Even the town lamps are in the shape of Hershey's Kisses. Much of the success of Hershey's was due to the company's ability to create and market new products that were, at the time, revolutionary. Milton Hershey was the first person to put nuts in candy bars, and the company developed special chocolates, using vegetable fats, that allowed wartime troops to take chocolate bars into combat situations in warm climates without melting, so soldiers could still enjoy the comforting and familiar flavor of chocolate far from home. The soldiers came home with fond remembrances of the Hershey chocolate bars that accompanied them into adverse situations.

Hershey, Pennsylvania, was modeled after the utopian vision created by Cadbury Chocolate in Bournville, England.

The town of Hershey became a model community for the citizens who worked for the chocolate factory and their families. Vowing to help the less privileged, Mr. Hershey built a school specifically for underprivileged children. After his death, the prime directive of the Hershey Trust (which owns the Hershey's chocolate company) was to endow and support the school. In 2002, the trust embarked on an attempt to sell the Hershey chocolate company, citing a need for steady income for the school, Mr. Hershey's prime directive. This move created a dilemma, as the mission of the trust was to support the school, not maintain ownership or the integrity of the chocolate company. Yet critics, and certainly employees, were furious, citing Mr. Hershey's intentions to keep Hershey's as an independent company. (Over the years, other companies, such as Ghirardelli and Godiva, had been bought out by larger corporations, with mixed results.) Eventually the trust decided against selling the company.

Scharffen Berger Chocolate

My introduction to Scharffen Berger chocolate was at a meeting for bakers in San Francisco. I was standing outside a bakery our group had toured, and a genial-enough fellow sidled up to me. I had no idea that this moment would change my life. He extracted a small packet wrapped in aluminum foil from his pocket. Since we were in a dicey neighborhood, perhaps I should have been a bit apprehensive, but he looked decent enough. He opened the crumpled foil to reveal a small gooey mass of something dark brown, sticky, and partially melted from the summer heat.

He asked me to sample it, and I can honestly say that it was the first time I really, truly understood what chocolate was all about. I recall being disarmingly intrigued; the chocolate was roasty and earthy, bittersweet, complex, with a coarse, unfinished edge that I found immensely appealing. I was tasting an experimental sample proffered by none other than Scharffen Berger's cofounder, Dr. Robert Steinberg.

He apologized for its coarseness, but his apologies were unnecessary. I was transfixed by his chocolate, although I thought he was out of his mind for starting a chocolate business. How could he compete in the big world of chocolate, with little more than a dream of changing the way America thinks about chocolate? I could not have been more wrong. Scharffen Berger has grown, prospered, and changed the public perception of chocolate, as well as the nature of the chocolate business in the United States.

Before John Scharffenberger and Robert Steinberg started producing their chocolate, I think most people in the United States were not well-informed about quality chocolate. It was often assumed that chocolate was either an industrial creation used to make a generally flavorless chocolate confection bought off a drugstore or supermarket shelf, or something exclusive and chic from Europe. Sometimes it was good, but often it was nothing more than a fancy label, promising more interesting flavors than the chocolate inside delivered.

Once their small-scale production was up and running, the publicity and interest they generated were immediate. Riding a renewed interest in American artisan foods, the last piece of the puzzle—chocolate—had been fitted into place. These two regular guys, John and Robert, worked in an undistinguished warehouse on the outskirts of San Francisco, using vintage European machinery, working day and night, roasting, grinding, and molding their deeply complex chocolate into glossy bars, each one handwrapped (they could not find a wrapping machine that would wrap such a small production of chocolate.) I had never realized that chocolate could be made with such passion and on such a personal level.

Robert traveled to South America to learn as much as he could about the cultivation and fermentation of cacao beans, and John, who previously owned a vineyard, learned about blending beans (similar to blending grapes) to bring out the best qualities of cacao. John Scharffenberger is hopeful that others in the United States will undertake similar, small-scale manufacturing of chocolate. He knows that if more people produce artisan chocolate, it will generate more attention and interest, and the entire industry will benefit from a heightened appreciation for quality chocolate.

As their popularity exploded, Scharffen Berger quickly outgrew their modest facilities and moved to a suitable brick building in Berkeley, California. The expanded factory, while still very small by industry standards, produces shiny tablets of dark chocolate in differing sizes, my favorite being the littlest ones with crunchy chopped cocoa nibs or coffee beans scattered throughout. Their organic cocoa powder is not Dutched (see page 36) since they believe that only inferior-quality cocoa powders need to be treated to have their acidity reduced. A visit to their website is almost as good as a visit to their factory, which can easily arranged through the site.

"From the bean to the bar" has been Scharffen Berger's motto, which defines their intention to educate an eager public about their careful procurement and roasting of the cacao beans, the subsequent blending and grinding, and the final depositing of this rich, thick liquid chocolate into molds to harden into their superb finished tablets of chocolate.

Scharffen Berger Chocolate Maker
914 Heinz Avenue
Berkeley, California 94710
1-800-930-4528
www.scharffenberger.com

THE FUTURE OF CHOCOLATE

From coarse beans being roasted over open fires for food, as well as being used as primitive currency, to ultrasleek modern factories churning out tons of chocolate each hour, the history of chocolate continues to evolve. What puzzles me now is that as we look back at how people enjoyed chocolate a century ago, we think how different the chocolate we consume today is than what was enjoyed just a century ago. So where will the future of chocolate take us? Can chocolate get any better?

International chocolate expert Chlöe Dontre-Roussel, chocolate buyer for Fortume Mason in London, believes that chocolate is headed in the same direction as coffee, and that some day we will buy it based on origin, plantation, and roast. American artisan John Scharffenberger thinks the technology may change, allowing chocolate makers to use a new process that enables the miniscule cacao particles to change in size, releasing yet even more different flavors in the finished chocolate. But then, if we knew what was going to be the next sensation in chocolate, wouldn't someone be doing it by now? Let's hope they're both right.

Christian Constant

CABOSSE
DE CACAO
7.00 €

Sustainability of Cacao

Nowhere is the deforestation and devastation of the planet's rain forests more evident than in the troubling patterns now seen in the cultivation of cacao. Cacao is a fragile crop. The tiny pink flowers that cover the branches of the cacao tree need to be pollinated, which is mostly done by small insects. This occurs naturally in a balanced rain forest ecosystem, but now, because the balance has been disrupted, hand pollination is often required.

As the popularity of chocolate increases each year, worldwide demand for cacao increases at a rate of about 3% annually. In West Africa, farmers are clearing land to grow cacao, deforesting the low-level trees while maintaining few of the higher trees, which provide necessary shade. The problem expands as eventually pests and disease strike these unprotected trees, and the farmers respond by clearing even more land for new cacao plantings. If growers and manufacturers are to keep up with increasing demand, it is vital that the rain forests remain as stable as possible so that the young cacao trees can thrive in their much-needed shade.

Some very large corporations, such as Cadbury's, Hershey's, Mars, and Nestlé, which depend on cacao for their confections, must confront the threat of the disappearing rain forests and the very real decreasing supply of cacao. And because the small-scale cacao farmers make very little money from their harvests, as opposed to the large profits of multinational corporations, international labor and conservation organizations, such as the World Cocoa Foundation (WCF, www.chocolateandcocoa.org), are working with both the corporations and the natives to achieve a mutually beneficial balance. The WCF is also leading the charge for tackling child labor practices in certain countries.

In addition to the threat of deforestation, cacao trees are subject to a variety of ailments, most notably witches' broom, a devastating spore that cannot be eliminated, or a fungus known as black pod rot, which infects the entire cacao tree. More than 75% of the Brazilian crop was destroyed by an infestation of witches' broom between the mid-1980s and 1998, apparently spread by human error. Even today nearly 25% of the annual cacao harvest is destroyed by the disease.

EVEN THE CHOCOLATE IS ORGANIC

Organic chocolate has been generating interest and enthusiasm and companies such as Chocolove (page 26), Dagoba (page 25), Newman's Own, and Rapunzel are contributing to the buzz with their entries in this part of the market. Even the highly regarded Barry-Callebaut chocolate collaborative of Belgium and France produces excellent dark, milk, and white chocolates made without pesticides or chemicals in accordance with strict European regulations.

In Berkeley, California, at the venerable Chez Panisse restaurant, organic chocolate is used exclusively in their desserts as part of the restaurant's commitment to sustainable agriculture. Pastry chef Alan Tangren uses Callebaut organic chocolate in chocolate desserts served in the formal dining room downstairs as well as the casual café upstairs, because "We wanted to know that our use of chocolate was not depleting the world's resources, but building them up. Tropical agriculture is right on that edge...so any practices that remove vegetation, such as clearing for large plantations, removes the fertility. Organic growers work within the existing forests, planting and tending the cacao trees in a way that maintains the health and productivity of the cacao trees." Desserts at Chez Panisse tend to be straightforward and uncomplicated, emphasizing just a few intense flavors, which makes the use of top-quality chocolate vital. Tangren believes that organic chocolate has a rich earthiness that works very well in this way, and says that the restaurant's customers often notice the difference.

The New Organic Chocolates

Certainly one of the most heartening trends in the story of chocolate is the nod to organics. As consumers have become more concerned about food sources, it was just a matter of time before chocolate makers began to respond.

Stop by any well-stocked grocer or natural food store and you'll find organic chocolate proudly displayed amongst the others. My favorite is Dagoba (www.dagoba chocolate.com). Unlike many other organic chocolate companies, which often farm out their production to larger manufacturers, Dagoba's equipment is used solely for producing organic chocolate. The youthful, spiky-haired founder, Frederick Schilling, has taken on the task of competing with the big manufacturers. However, instead of making the usual chocolate-and-nut bars, Frederick has created an enticing palette of flavors for his chocolates. But his pure milk chocolate bar, with 35% cacao solids, has the freshest dairy flavor I've encountered in a milk chocolate, organic or otherwise. Dagoba also adroitly blends the zing of spiced tea into his chocolate to create a chai bar. I detected notes of smoky cardamom, the subtle warmth of black pepper, and a dusting of nutmeg plus the zip of candied ginger. If only they'd manufacture a hot chocolate mix using these flavors!

For a zesty tropical tornado of flavor, try the Dagoba Lime Bar. Peeling back the wrapper, the tang of lime zest zoomed into my senses. The combination of bright lime, dark chocolate, and nubbins of crushed macadamias was so good I couldn't stop eating the darned thing! Other bars made by Dagoba include a ruddy dark chocolate with 74% cacao, another with 55% cacao, and the "Brasilia" milk chocolate bar with roasted Brazil nuts and shredded coconut. Like cacao, Brazil nuts are a product of the rain forest, and their consumption provides economic stimulus for preservation of the rain forest.

Another widely distributed organic chocolate is Chocolove (www.chocolove.com). Imported from Belgium, Chocolove makes two different organic chocolate bars: a 61% and a 73%. Chocolove chocolates are from Caribbean-grown beans. Curiously, I found the 61% to have much more chocolate flavor. It danced in my mouth with lots of candylike floral notes, finishing with a smooth, lingering chocolate taste. The 73% was more direct, although when I tasted it with Lindsey Shere, author of *Chez Panisse Desserts*, and her husband, Charles, they preferred the 73% and felt that it left a much longer, rounder chocolate impression.

Yet the most unusual chocolate product that I have ever had is Yachana Jungle Chocolate (www.yachana.com). Yachana's organic cacao nibs are not processed into chocolate bars. Instead, the crunchy bits are dipped in Amazon cane syrup, sometimes with pineapple juice, creating one of the most intriguing, delectable, and original chocolate taste sensations that I've ever had. A newer blend has finely diced macadamia nuts added. Not only is Yachana Jungle Chocolate organic, but the farmers who supply the chocolate maker are paid much more than the local market price, encouraging them to continue to grow cacao instead of crops that generate more profit, such as cocaine. All profits from Yachana Jungle Chocolate support health care projects for native Ecuadorian people.

A STEP IN THE WRONG DIRECTION

In 2000, the European Union introduced a directive, allowing companies to replace up to 5% of the cocoa butter in their chocolates with vegetable fat and still call it chocolate. This has enraged purists who see the policy change as the ruination of chocolate's purity amid increasing doubts about the healthfulness of added tropical, often hydrogenated, fats. A vocal opponent was Chantal Coady, author of *Real Chocolate* and the proprietor of Rococo Chocolates (www.rococo.ro) in London. In addition to the possible harm to one's health from ingesting these added tropical fats, she points out that these

the great book of chocolate

chocolates "Do not melt properly and leave a greasy coating on the palate." After intense criticism, the European Union amended its directive so that chocolate products with added fats other than cocoa butter must state clearly on the label: "Contains vegetable fats in addition to cocoa butter," and in Great Britain, it must be labeled as "family chocolate."

Because cacao products, including cocoa butter, are essential to the economies of many underdeveloped countries, farmers on the Ivory Coast of Africa have cultivated shea trees that provide a tropical fat similar to the cocoa butter used in the confectionery and cosmetic industries. (Mango seed and palm kernel oils are among other tropical fats used in these industries.)

Promoting purity in our food sources is an easy way to effect change each time we shop. Tampering with nature by adding other fats to chocolate may make money, but for chocolate lovers, altering something so intrinsically perfect with cheaper fats doesn't make sense. I never buy chocolate based on price, only on quality.

We need to be truly conscious about where our food comes from and how its cultivation affects the environment. Buying (and eating!) more chocolate gives manufactures a powerful economic incentive to preserve the ecological balance of cacao-bearing rain forests. Fine organic chocolates are now available in response to the world's growing interest in sustainable agriculture. And not only are organic and sustainable chocolate manufacturers responding to environmental concerns, they're providing even greater variety and more choices for chocolate aficionados.

A Chocolate Primer

The determinants of the final flavor of the chocolate are the growing and harvesting the beans, the proper fermentation and drying, the blending of beans to achieve a flavor profile, and the subsequent roasting and conching. In most cases, the beans are processed far from their place of origin, so the actual geographical location of the factory that turns them into chocolate is of little consequence. For example, beans grown and fermented in Africa might be shipped to Belgium to be roasted, ground, and molded into chocolate. And there is nothing about, say, the environment in Europe that makes the factories there produce better chocolate. If excellent-quality beans were shipped to Antarctica for chocolate production, there's no reason that factories there couldn't produce top-quality chocolate. Consequently Belgian- and French-made chocolates are not necessarily better or more flavorful than American-made chocolate, or chocolates made anywhere else. (That said, certain countries, such as Belgium, do have a tradition of producing excellent chocolate and consequently much of the chocolate from Belgium *is* excellent.) We should retrain ourselves not to use the country of manufacture as a barometer of quality.

WHAT'S IN A NAME?

To confuse matters just a bit more, there are different classifications of chocolate, from unsweetened chocolate liquor to cocoa butter–rich white chocolate, which, in some places, is not legally classified as chocolate at all. Following are definitions and descriptions of all the most common varieties of chocolate or chocolate products that you'll come across. There's also information and descriptions of contemporary terms such as "single-origin" and "single-bean," now being used to classify chocolates as well. Once you understand this information, you'll be able to identify chocolates and understand their differences as well as the similarities.

Baking Chocolate

You will sometimes encounter "baking chocolate" in the United States and Europe. Baking chocolate is sold in bars that are, in general, about 60% cacao paste and 40% sugar. Since they are intended for baking only, not confectionery, there is no added cocoa butter. Bonnat (page 33) produces a good one.

the great book of chocolate

Baking-Resistant Chocolate

Most of us are familiar with baking-resistant chocolate in the form of semisweet chocolate morsels. These chips are considered "baking-resistant" because they retain their shape during the heat of baking due to the decreased amount of cocoa butter added to the chocolate. Baking-resistant chocolate, such as semisweet chocolate morsels, in general should *not* be melted and used in place of bittersweet or semisweet chocolate as the lower amount of cocoa butter will result in a very thick, somewhat unworkable mass.

Several manufacturers have introduced baking chips and pieces that are to be used in place of chocolate morsels; the best, such as Callebaut, Ghirardelli, Guittard, and Nestlé chunks, are made from better-quality chocolate.

Compound "Chocolate" Coating

Not chocolate at all, compound chocolate-flavored coatings contain sugar, cocoa powder, vegetable fat, and sometimes chocolate liquor and cocoa butter. These inexpensive and inferior-tasting coatings are vegetable-based and designed for enrobing cakes and candies that may be subjected to high heat (which is why they are sometimes labeled "summer coating"), which can cause the cocoa butter to separate and bloom (page 38). The appeal of using compound coating is that it eliminates the need to temper the chocolate, as there is little cocoa butter to separate. If you have to use compound chocolate, look for a brand with cocoa butter or chocolate liquor as an ingredient. Sometimes they are deceptively identified as "chocolate-flavored" coating. The best use for compound chocolate is for making chocolate decorations, which are used mostly for appearance and less likely to be savored .

Couverture

In general, couverture, or "coating chocolate" is semisweet or bittersweet chocolate with extra cocoa butter added. The extra cocoa butter improves the texture and fluidity, and is often preferred by professional confectioners and pastry chefs for enrobing. Many premium brands of bittersweet and semisweet chocolate are considered couverture even though they are not labeled as such.

Flavored "Chocolate"

Sold primarily to professional confectioners, flavored chocolates are made by compounding dark, milk, or white chocolate with a flavoring, such as roasted coffee beans, nuts, dried fruits, or natural citrus oils. Some of these are very good and others may contain artificial flavors. Check the list of ingredients. Search for brands with natural flavorings and colors.

Gianduja

Gianduja refers to milk or dark chocolate compounded during the manufacture with roasted hazelnuts, popular in Europe. *Gianduja* is blended so it's absolutely smooth, then formed into a solid block, resembling pure chocolate.

Ground Chocolate

Although ground chocolate resembles cocoa powder, it's actually pulverized sweetened chocolate. And since it contains sugar, it is mostly used to make chocolate drinks and should not be used in place of unsweetened cocoa powder in recipes as it is a very different product.

Milk Chocolate

Milk chocolate must contain a minimum of 10% cacao solids and 12% milk solids (dried). Sugar is always added and usually a small amount of lecithin as well. Some manufacturers use lightly caramelized milk solids and others use dried condensed milk, which can give the milk chocolate a faint taste of scalded milk. Premium brands of milk chocolate, often labeled "dark milk chocolate" usually contain up to 48% cacao solids or more. Milk chocolate will keep in a cool, dark place for up to 18 months.

As Dark As Milk Chocolate Gets

The darkest milk chocolate I've ever had is made by Bonnat (www.bonnat-chocolatier.com), in the town of Voiron, in the Savoy region of France. With such exotic names as Asfarth, Java (my favorite), and Surabaya, Bonnat milk chocolate bars contain a whopping 65% cacao solids. Unlike other chocolatiers, Bonnat does not put vanilla or lecithin in their chocolates; their reasoning is that vanilla interferes with the chocolate flavor and that more modern conching (mixing) techniques make the emulsifier lecithin unnecessary.

Bonnat also makes a superb line of bittersweet chocolate bars that they call their Grand Crus du Cacao: Puerto Cabello and El Rosario from Venezuela, Equator from South America, Madagascar from the Indian Ocean, and Trinité bars from the Antilles. Should you visit the region, a favorite of mine in southeast France, Voiron is also the location of the world-famous Chartreuse distillery (Bonnat makes chocolates filled with liquid Chartreuse that are to die for). The Bonnat family welcomes visitors to tour their chocolate factory, which can be arranged through their website.

Semisweet and Bittersweet Chocolate

Both must contain a minimum of 35% cacao solids. In addition, sugar is added for sweetness and cocoa butter for fluidity and smooth mouthfeel. Lecithin is often added and sometimes vanilla or vanillin, an artificial vanilla made from pine tree resin. In spite of what you may hear, semisweet and bittersweet chocolate are interchangeable terms. Sweetness and bitterness are determined by the manufacturer, so unless the recipe specifies, you can use one in place of the other. Interestingly, dark chocolates often improve greatly by allowing several months after manufacture for aging, which provides a chance for the flavors to mellow. Sometimes very fresh chocolate has a slightly green or unripe character. Semisweet and bittersweet chocolate will keep in a cool, dark place for 3 to 5 years.

Dark versus Milk

As a professional chef, I'm always curious about what motivates people to choose a specific taste over another one. I was puzzled for many years by people who prefer sweet milk chocolate over bittersweet dark chocolate. To me, dark chocolate has much more flavor. And more flavor is always better, right?

This question plagued me for years until I found my answer in the village of Louviers, in Normandy, France.

While cooking with chef and author Susan Herrmann Loomis, I met a woman who could not eat anything with strong flavors. To her, eating something as puckery as a grapefruit, raspberries, or even drinking red wine (which is tannic) was overwhelming.

I researched and learned that some people are what scientists call "supertasters," the manifestation of a trait that's determined genetically. Different parts of the tongue register different flavors: the front of the tongue senses sweet, while the sides detect bitter. Supertasters have a highly perceptive or altered sense of taste, which accounts for why some people find dark bittersweet chocolate (or spicy or bitter foods) too strongly flavored to enjoy. Supertasters are characterized by having an overwhelming number of taste buds in their mouths. A low-tech method of counting taste buds is sometimes used: adhesive circles known as "reinforcements" (disks to protect the holes in notebook paper), are used to manually count taste buds. Supertasters have 30 taste buds within an area, whereas "nontasters" (people with little taste sensation) have about 5 taste buds within the same area. It is estimated that between 10% and 35% of the population are supertasters, a phenomenon more common in women. Scientists fear that being a supertaster may increase the risk of cancer, since many cancer-fighting foods have bitter characteristics that taste disagreeable to supertasters. Many supermodels, who are very lean, are also thought to be supertasters and don't crave flavor.

But if you happen to be someone like me who loves very bitter chocolate (and not a supermodel), the bar for you is the Chocolat Noir Infini 99% made by Michel Cluizel of France (available at www.chocosphere.com). This slender 30-gram bar, almost black in color, is 99% cacao solids with a teeny amount of sugar added, plus a whisper of orange blossom and spice. Very similar to unsweetened chocolate, this beguiling bar is best enjoyed by placing a small piece between your tongue and the roof of your mouth and letting it dissolve rather than chewing it, allowing you to savor the bitter flavor of the chocolate; chewing releases too much of the bitterness.

Single-Origin and Estate Chocolates

Single-origin chocolates, which are made from the cacao beans of one site, are of somewhat recent interest. These chocolates are often named after the actual regions in which the cacao beans were grown, such as Arriba, Ecuador, Java, and Sur del Lago. Yet another specialized category is estate chocolate, which is made from beans grown on one particular estate. However, because one estate may grow several varieties of cacao beans, often this term is meaningless.

Sweet Chocolate

More of a snacking confection and rarely used in baking, products labeled as sweet chocolate must contain at least 15% cacao solids. Most of us are familiar with the Ibarra brand, a sweet chocolate made in Mexico, sometimes ground with peanuts or almonds and cinnamon, specially blended for Mexican-style hot chocolate.

Unsweetened Cocoa Powder

Unsweetened cocoa power is made from warm chocolate liquor (unsweetened chocolate paste), which is slammed through a powerful hydraulic press, separating the cocoa solids from the cocoa butter. What remains in the press after the cocoa butter is removed is a very hard, dense compressed disk of cocoa. The expelled ivory-colored cocoa butter is either saved to be added to other chocolate products, or sold to the cosmetic and pharmaceutical industries, where it is used for lipsticks, body creams, and suppositories. (Cocoa butter can be deodorized to remove any chocolate smell, and its melting point, about 97°F [36°C], makes it ideal for smooth application to the skin. In addition, cocoa butter is fairly resistant to oxidation and spoilage.) The rock-hard compressed cocoa cake is crushed and pulverized into natural cocoa powder. Depending on how much cocoa butter is extracted during the pressing, cocoa powders for baking contain between 10% and 22% fat. Cocoa powders labeled "low fat" contain less than 10% fat. Low-fat baking often relies on cocoa powder because it contains the flavor of chocolate with much of the fat removed.

When cocoa powder has been "Dutched," it means that the cocoa powder (or cacao nibs before they are ground) have been washed with a harmless alkali solution of potassium carbonate to neutralize the acidity and darken the powder. Most traditional American recipes call for non-Dutched cocoa powder along with the use of baking soda as a leavening agent. A general rule for baking recipes is that Dutched cocoa is used in recipes that use acidic baking powder, but recipes that use baking soda, which is alkali, should use natural cocoa powder. An example of how cocoa powder reacts with alkali liquids is the classic Black-Bottom Cupcakes (page 104). When you make devil's food cake, it gets its devilish red tinge from the reaction caused by the baking soda alkalizing the natural cocoa powder, so you would not use Dutched cocoa powder.

Regarding the interchangeability of Dutched and non-Dutched cocoa powders in recipes, food scientist Harold McGee, author of *On Food and Cooking: The Science and Lore of the Kitchen*, explains that eggs neutralize the pH in most batters, so if eggs are included, either type of cocoa powder may be used. I always recommend using what the recipe indicates and, when in doubt, follow McGee's rule: don't worry about it, but use a good, flavorful brand. Sometimes you'll notice that recipes using cocoa powder call for mixing the cocoa powder with hot liquid before adding it to the batter. This causes the cocoa flavor to "bloom" and become fuller and richer.

Black cocoa (available from King Arthur Flour) is highly alkalized cocoa powder. It's most commonly consumed in Oreo cookies, which have a dark, dusky chocolate flavor and almost black color. Although lacking in rich chocolate flavor, some bakers like to add a percentage of black cocoa with regular cocoa powder to intensify the darkness.

Unsweetened or Bitter Chocolate

Unsweetened chocolate usually contains 100% cacao solids, although it may have less than 1% lecithin, a soy-based emulsifier. Unsweetened chocolate is solid "chocolate liquor," cacao beans ground to a smooth paste with no added sugar or fat and usually sold as a hardened block. In Europe, you'll find unsweetened chocolate referred to as *pâte de cacao* (cocoa paste). Unsweetened chocolate will keep in a cool, dark place for up to 5 years.

White Chocolate

Not officially (or legally) chocolate because it has no cacao solids, ivory-colored white chocolate is made from cocoa butter and sugar, with added dairy solids and sometimes vanilla or vanillin. It's important to use the best brands since the quality of white chocolate is almost entirely dependent on the aroma and taste of the rich cocoa butter. Avoid products labeled as "white confectioner coating" and the like, which contain little, if any, cocoa butter and are suspiciously pure white instead of ivory-colored. A glance at the list of ingredients is all that's necessary to make sure cocoa butter is the only fat used and you're getting the real thing. Inferior brands have vegetable oils or other tropical fats. White chocolate will keep in a cool, dark place for up to 12 months.

HOW TO STORE SOLID CHOCOLATE

All solid baking and confectionery chocolates are best stored at a temperature between 60°F and 70°F (16°C and 21°C) with a maximum of 50% humidity. Air, light, and humidity are all to be avoided. Do not store chocolate in the refrigerator, where moisture levels are high. And don't store it near anything with a strong smell since chocolate absorbs surrounding odors.

What Is Tempering?

Tempering is the most vexing task for most home bakers and chocolatiers. Chocolate is composed of cocoa fat and sugar crystals. Before melted chocolate is cooled and solidified, the fats need to be emulsified. Otherwise the cocoa butter will rise to the surface and form gray streaks. Think of a vinaigrette dressing that is well-shaken, but upon standing, separates into distinct layers of oil and vinegar, or meat stock, which upon cooling has a layer of fat solidified on the surface. So chocolatiers must temper their chocolate if it's to be used as a coating. Tempering stabilizes the crystals to prevent fat "bloom," the whitish gray streaks that appear on the surface of untempered chocolate or on chocolate that has been tempered but stored in a warm environment. Although unattractive and unappealing, untempered chocolate with gray streaks is not at all harmful to eat.

When you unwrap a bar of chocolate, it should be smooth, glossy, and snap cleanly where you break it. When you touch the chocolate, it will not melt on contact with your fingers. Tempering chocolate raises the temperature at which chocolate melts, so it doesn't soften and leave an impression when you touch it. Tempering gives chocolate its snap, the result of having created a microscopic honeycomb texture. In addition, tempered chocolate contracts just a bit as it's cooling, allowing chocolatiers to easily remove filled chocolates from metal or polycarbonate chocolate molds. If you are ever fortunate enough to visit a chocolate production facility, you can hear a chorus of crackling as tempered chocolate that's been deposited into molds cools, shrinks, and releases from the molds.

Chocolate is tempered

- To avoid fat and sugar bloom, characterized by unappealing gray streaks, crystals, or blotches on the surface.

- To raise the melting temperature of hardened chocolate so it does not melt on contact with hands.

- To make melted chocolate contract slightly once it's cooled for easy release from decorative molds.

- To preserve the keeping quality of chocolate by emulsifying the fat.

- To cool chocolate quickly. Tempered chocolate cools usually within about 5 minutes, depending on the temperature, and the quantity and thickness of the chocolate.

- To give chocolate a glossy, shiny appearance and a crisp, clean breaking quality.

HOW TO STORE FILLED CHOCOLATE CONFECTIONS

The best filled chocolates, such as truffles and bonbons, have shelf lives of only about 1 to 2 weeks at room temperature. Because the fillings are often made with fresh cream and butter, their perishability is the trade-off for delicacy. So don't feel guilty indulging impatiently in a box of premium-quality chocolates—they are a fleeting pleasure, meant to be consumed with a bit of urgency!

Many mass-produced or commercial chocolates keep longer, sometimes up to 2 months. Often they are made with sterilized dairy products that have a much longer shelf life. Be sure to notice any tiny cracks or fissures with oozing or frothy filling, which is usually an indication of spoilage.

If you're not going to enjoy your chocolates soon enough, you can enclose the entire package in a heavy-duty zip-top freezer bag and store them in the freezer for 2 to 3 months. Chocolates can also be stored in the refrigerator for up to 1 month. Either way there may be a nominal decline in quality. If you do chill your chocolates, be sure to allow them to come to room temperature at least 1 hour before serving, so they will soften and have the proper texture, allowing the flavors to come forward.

Filled chocolates are also prone to scratching, which is why chocolatiers take great pains to cushion their chocolate. Take care to store uneaten chocolates in their original packaging and avoid piling them on top of one another.

FINISH
YOUR
MILK

Chocolate and Wellness

Modern medicine is just beginning to catch on to something that the tribes of long ago practiced: using chocolate for medicinal purposes. Research has shown that although cocoa butter is high in saturated fat, it does not raise cholesterol levels due to its high stearic acid content, which some believe lowers the level of serum cholesterol. Other studies show that chocolate contains polyphenols, which may thin the blood and prevent oxidation in the blood flow, inhibiting the bad cholesterol (LDL) that is believed to build up plaque in the arteries and restrict blood flow. Still other medical studies have concluded that cacao contains ingredients similar to those in mind-altering drugs and over-the-counter anti-depressants.

Centuries ago, cacao was used as a disinfectant, its flowers were used to alleviate apathy, and the milky white pulp was used to facilitate birth. Later, most commonly in Europe during the past two centuries, chocolate was classified as a drug and dispensed in pharmacies to those with weak constitutions or symptoms of fatigue and malaise. The small disks of "medicinal" chocolate were scented and flavored with vanilla and orange flowers. Their consumption was said to aid health and digestion, although classifying chocolate as a drug also helped people avoid paying taxes on it because virtually everything but medications was taxable. We may think of this as strange, but consider the panoply of chocolate-flavored calcium and weight-loss supplements (not to mention chocolate-flavored Ex-Lax), all chocolafied to get adults to take their medicine.

Debauve & Gallais (page 78), a former pharmacy, still operates a splendid chocolate shop in Paris, selling disks of dark chocolate coyly labeled to allude to their past as an antidote for whatever ails you.

Top Antioxidant Foods	*ORAC**
	Units per 100 grams
Dark Chocolate	13,120
Milk Chocolate	6,740
Prunes	5,770
Raisins	2,830
Blueberries	2,400
Blackberries	2,036
Kale	1,770
Strawberries	1,540
Spinach	1,260
Raspberries	1,220
Brussels Sprouts	980
Plums	949
Alfalfa Sprouts	930
Broccoli Florets	890
Oranges	750
Red Grapes	739
Red Bell Peppers	710
Cherries	670
Onions	450
Corn	400
Eggplant	390

*Oxygen Radical Absorbance Capacity (ORAC) is a measure of the ability of the food to subdue harmful oxygen free radicals that can damage our bodies. Source: Data from the U.S. Department of Agriculture and the *Journal of the American Chemical Society* .

Researchers continue to uncover startling facts about cacao. Amazingly, cacao beans are shown to have the highest amount of antioxidants of any known plant source—much greater than highly touted prunes and even red wine, the darling of the French Paradox. Antioxidants suppress free radicals, which can damage healthy cells in your body. Consequently, eating dark chocolate, which contains more cacao solids, would be healthier for you than eating milk chocolate.

IS CHOCOLATE A DRUG?

Studies have shown that chocolate contains theobromine, phenylethylamine (PEA), anandamide, and cannabinoids, which are similar to the mind-altering components found in the drugs ecstasy and marijuana. People with depression tend to consume more chocolate than others, perhaps due to the presence of these chemicals. And PEA has a similar effect on the chemistry of the brain to what we experience when we fall in love.

Chocolate's high level of magnesium (131 mg per 100 grams) is credited for adding to the euphoria one gets from eating chocolate. And serotonin (3 mg per 100 grams) and tyramine (2 mg per 100 grams) are also present in chocolate and provide a mild calming, balancing effect. Most chocolate lovers don't need scientists to tell them that chocolate is indeed mood altering, but perhaps scientists have discovered medical grounds for our addiction (and now we can all feel better about eating chocolate).

Bottoms Up!

An enterprising company in Great Britain is marketing a tasty little chocolate beverage called Positively Healthy Cocoa Drink, which I discovered at Harrod's in London. One little bottle, about 3 ounces, has as many natural antioxidants as approximately 1 pound of blueberries, apples, or red grapes, or half a bottle of red wine.

Marketed by the Positive Food Company (www.healthy cocoa.com), they claim that their particular cocoa is specially processed to retain 100% of the natural antioxidants that most other cocoas lose during processing. The drink is delicious; I'd have no trouble drinking a bottle— or more—a day.

It has been disproved that chocolate causes acne (teenagers rejoice!) and we know that there is only a small amount of caffeine in chocolate: a 1-ounce piece of milk chocolate contains 6 milligrams of caffeine, the equivalent of a cup of decaffeinated coffee. A 1-ounce piece of dark chocolate has 10 to 20 milligrams of caffeine; 1 cup of regular coffee has 100 to 120 milligrams of caffeine.

In spite of claims in the early 1900s that milk chocolate is healthy for you (Cadbury's proudly boasted a whopping "1¹/2 glasses of English full cream milk in every half pound!), I doubt that anyone would say that you'd be better off nutritionally to eat a half pound of milk chocolate than drinking a glass of fresh milk. Nutrient-enriched chocolate drinks, such as Ovaltine and Banania (a European beverage made with banana flour), were also developed and marketed to persuade parents to feed their children chocolate with their milk since vitamins and minerals were included in the mixture and it got children to drink their milk.

Dr. Robert Steinberg, co-founder of Scharffen Berger chocolate, believes that the least-fermented chocolate has the most polyphenols (which raise the antioxidant level).

Although less-fermented chocolate may be the highest in tannins, it's not the best quality for eating. Steinberg is convinced that the proper fermentation of the cacao beans is the most important step in high-quality chocolate production, so consequently the best quality cacao does not have the highest amounts of antioxidants. "Look, it's wishful thinking to imagine that eating chocolate is going make you healthy," he explains, "but pure dark chocolate made with relatively little sugar is pure food, food that comes from the earth, and minimally processed to maintain the purity of the seed of a tropical fruit. Chocolate is not the magic potion that people are searching for…chocolate is basically a reasonable component of a balanced diet."

If you want to enjoy whatever health benefits chocolate may have, research suggests that the greatest benefits come from dark chocolate, which contains a high proportion of cacao solids, namely unsweetened, bittersweet, and semisweet chocolate. Of course, medical opinions and research data change over time, so it is somewhat of a stretch for anyone to consume large amounts of chocolate in an effort to get healthy. But next time you bite into a bar of bittersweet chocolate, you may be rewarding your body as well as your taste buds.

Buying Chocolate

You walk into a chocolate shop. You see rows and rows of gorgeous chocolates for sale. The salesperson waits behind the counter for you to decide. You get a little nervous. You ponder. You think. You carefully consider this important decision. All the chocolates beckon. What do you do?

For too many of us, buying chocolate is a special event. Or we buy chocolate already packaged, depriving us the freedom to mix and match according to our passions. Do you like dark or light? How about creamy centers? Do you want simple ganache-filled truffles or more complex centers? Nuts?

But what do you do if you're confronted with such a difficult choice in an elegant chocolate boutique in the United States, or a fashionable salon of chocolate confections abroad, where shopping for chocolates is an art?

TIPS FOR CHOCOLATE BUYERS

1. As you enter the shop, look to confirm that it's clean and orderly—it certainly should be. The best chocolatiers are fanatical about quality, hygiene, and appearance, and are proud of their creations, working very diligently to present them properly. The salesperson will often put on a white cotton glove to handle the chocolates. This does not mean their hands are dirty; it's to avoid getting their fingerprints on your chocolates.

2. Note the condition of the chocolates. Small bubbles on the upper edges indicate that when the chocolates were being molded, the molds were not properly agitated to release the air. While this is a small flaw, it is a reflection on the chocolate maker's level of care and precision.

3. Check to see that the chocolates have no cracks. Cracks mean either that the fillings that were dipped were too cold or overfilled, or that the chocolates are old. If there is filling bubbling and oozing out, it means that the insides were not hygienically prepared before being enrobed and they're spoiled. If the cracks are the result of cold filling, there is the possibility that the center may have suffered in quality, as a solid chocolate coating provides a protective case for the enclosed filling.

4. When ordering individual chocolates to be arranged in a box to your specifications by a salesperson, always choose the flattest chocolates first rather than those that are tall or shapely. Requesting the flat ones first means that the subsequent layer(s) will be easier to pack and arrive at their destination in better condition. The chocolates on the bottom won't get damaged, and having the variety of shapes and sizes on top makes the box more attractive upon opening.

5. Handle the chocolates with care after you take them from the shop. Store them properly in a cool, dark place until you eat them (see storage guidelines, page 39).

the great book of chocolate

A "MARKET" APPROACH
TO FINE CHOCOLATE-MAKING

When I went to artisan candy maker Michael Recchiuti's workshop, located in a large loft in a secluded quarter of San Francisco, he was leaning over the sink sloshing something around under water. Unusual for a chocolatier, I thought. As I got closer, I noticed he was dunking vivid green bunches of organic lemon verbena, which he explained he had just purchased at the organic farmers' market a few hours before. This typifies Michael Recchiuti's approach to confections: searching for the best ingredients, taking them back to his workshop, and coaxing their flavors into his brilliant chocolates.

As Michael told me, he never worries about people stealing his ideas or trying to re-create what he does. "My chocolates are so labor-intensive, no one would ever copy them," he jokes. He tenderly removed a chocolate from its mold for me to taste. A long, slender white chocolate confection, tipped with a crisp line of dark chocolate and dusted with a dreamy shower of gold dust. As I bit into it, the balmy aroma took over my senses. Inside was the powerful essence of rose geranium combined with caramel, which was cooked just beyond what most people would consider prudent. Smoky, sweet, and just a touch burnt. In short, exactly the way perfect caramel is supposed to taste, but rarely does. It brilliantly offset the sweet richness of the white chocolate used to enrobe the candy. I've never met a chocolatier like Michael Recchiuti, who works like a chef, foraging for his ingredients at the local markets, combining them with the exotic chocolates he discovers around the world. Pungent and sweet herbs, ripe fruits, smoky teas, and seasonal flower essences all find their way into his chocolate confections.

In spite of how sophisticated Michael's chocolates may sound, he has a playful side, which is seen in his re-creations of favorite childhood treats, including the densest slabs of brownies, S'mores with his pillowy marshmallows and homemade graham crackers, and gooey Whoopy Pies. And when he's not in his workshop creating his delightful confections, Michael rises early for the San Francisco Ferry Plaza Farmer's Market, where he likes to search for yet more ingredients and inspiration. Michael also likes to "put a face on his chocolates" by attending the market personally, talking and answering questions, and then seeing the ecstatic look on his customers' faces as they sample his handiwork.

I, too, have been thrilled by Michael's confections. His brownies are both rich and chewy, with all the qualities of the best brownies your mom never made. His take on the traditional Pennsylvania Dutch Whoopie Pie brilliantly transforms the treat into a sophisticated confection with soft marshmal-

Michael Recchiuti in his workshop.

low tucked between devil's food cake, encased in very dark Guittard Sur de Lago chocolate. His all-American peanut butter cups are filled with creamy organic peanut butter layered between El Rey Venezuelan dark milk chocolate, a fleck of fleur de sel added to provide exactly the right lingering finish. Although all his "snacks" (as he calls them) and filled chocolates are made with the freshest ingredients, his dark chocolate tablets fabricated from a proprietary blend of cacao beans are perfect for gift giving or just nibbling yourself. One is made from ground roasted hazelnuts flecked with *feuilletine*, crispy, tiny bits of crunchy cookies, and another envelops soft honey nougat with bits of roasted California almonds.

Michael was fortunate enough to study with a mentor, Alain Tricou, and he still has scars to prove it, pointing to a long indentation in his forehead courtesy of a flying skillet. (The best chefs always throw things.) Yet this experience was vital to his growth. After they'd toil in the workshop all day, they'd linger together later at home, pulling sugar into whimsical shapes just for the fun of it. Michael was an eager student, lucky to learn from the master of confectionery, provided he was able to overlook the occasional tantrum or airborne piece of cookware.

Michael has also created an exciting collection of filled chocolates with brilliantly realized flavors such as sesame nougat, star anise and pink peppercorn ganache, cardamom combined with cacao nibs, tangy tarragon and grapefruit, and honeycomb malt. He even imports his own Holualoa coffee beans directly from Kona, which he searched out since these particular Kona coffee beans "work with the chocolate, not against it." This theme carries through as he melds his skills as a master chocolatier with artisan sensibilities, demonstrated by his ability to redefine classics and create new ones with a modern palette of flavors and tastes. Although his confections have a handmade quality, they are flawless in both their taste and appearance and excite all the senses with their sleek presentation and well-executed combination of flavors and textures.

Recchiuti Confections

San Francisco Ferry Building Marketplace
One Ferry Building, Shop #30
San Francisco, California 94111
1-800-500-3396
www.recchiutichocolates.com

A SAN FRANCISCO TREAT

My first experience with Guittard was when I began baking professionally over 25 years ago. I had never heard of Guittard chocolate, located just south of San Francisco, and when I began unwrapping, chopping, melting, and tasting Guittard chocolate, I was involuntarily drawn into the world of fine chocolate. That was a defining moment for me as a chocolate lover and pastry chef.

Guittard chocolate was a revelation, and it was the first time that I had a dark chocolate epiphany. At the time, Guittard did not make their chocolates available to the public because most of it was used by professionals, who already knew a thing or two about chocolate. (See's candy company, another California favorite that's located just down the street, has Guittard's still-liquid chocolate shipped to their factory and poured directly into their chocolate-coating machines.)

Guittard Chocolate Company was founded in 1868 by Etienne Guittard, whose name appears in the first telephone directory in San Francisco (which was one page!). Much has changed in the world of chocolate since then, but Guittard is still family owned and operated, with fourth-generation family member Gary Guittard at the helm. These days Guittard is using their extensive knowledge and research to create new chocolates for the chocolate lover to snack on and for home baking.

I was among the first to taste the vintage chocolates marketed under the E. Guittard label. Some are blends of up to seven different beans and others are single-bean varietals with 65% cacao mass. Of the single-bean varietals, the Sur del Lago was exceptional. Sweet, fruity, cherrylike flavors contrasted with an intense roasted cacao bitterness. Sur del Lago cacao is one of the rarest and finest cacao beans, and in the hands of these master chocolate makers, it yields a truly exceptional chocolate. Two other single-bean varietals, Columbian and Ecuador Nacional, are both from *trinitario* beans. The Columbian chocolate has an espresso-like flavor that is mildly acidic and just a tad spicy. It would be perfect in a dessert served with coffee. When I close my eyes, the Ecuador has the spicy astringency reminiscent of a young Cabernet wine.

I also enjoyed their blends, which included the wonderful L'Harmonie, a 64% dark chocolate, which has become one of my favorite chocolates and the one I use in my brownie recipes when bittersweet chocolate is called for. It is an excellent all-around chocolate. The Coucher du Soleil (which means "sunset") has 72% cacao mass and is dark and rich with a crisp, clean chocolate flavor.

Guittard also makes chocolate "chunks" with their superior quality chocolate. The chunks are better for baking than most commercial semisweet chips because they're made from chocolate designed to melt into gooey chunks rather than holding their shapes as firm chips. Premium-quality E. Guittard chocolates are now available to chocolate lovers and home bakers.

Guittard Chocolate

1-800-468-2462
www.guittard.com

Where's All That Chocolate Going?

The largest consumers of chocolate are the Swiss, who eat 21 pounds (9.5 kg) a year per person, with Great Britain following at a close second at 18 pounds (8.2 kg) per person annually. Citizens of the United States consume 12 pounds (5.4 kg) a year and although the Belgians produce much of the world's supply of chocolate, they enjoy only about 16 pounds (7.3 lg) of chocolate per person each year.

Zaventem, Brussels's international airport in Belgium, is the world's largest chocolate shop, selling over 500 tons of chocolate each year. October is the most popular month for buying chocolate there, followed by December.

SURFING A WAVE OF CHOCOLATE

Richard Donnelly has the ultimate "what I did on my summer vacation" story. In the mid-1980s, he was living in New England and his brother was living near Santa Cruz, a sleepy yet energized and politically charged seaside community that epitomizes the California surfing lifestyle. While visiting his brother, Richard saw a for-sale ad for the workshop of a failed caramel apple business. On a whim, he bought the workshop and relocated to Santa Cruz, opening a chocolate shop in the modest location.

Unlike many other chocolate shops, Richard's cannot be considered slick or lavish. There are not a lot of gleaming racks of sparkling utensils or fancy equipment. There are only amazing chocolates being made on every counter and in every corner, all by hand. There seem to be at least a dozen projects going on at once, with Richard alternating between several, as he checks his tempered chocolate and waits on customers simultaneously. And just for fun, Richard produces a few sundries made from chocolate; soothing eye pillows filled with cacao beans, tubes of chocolate lip balm (which you just have to try to believe), and homemade soap with nuggets of cacao within. A simple handwritten sign lets you know what dipped chocolates are currently available. This is not a factory, it's Richard Donnelly's world of chocolate, and his are better than just about any chocolates you've ever had.

Instead of spending his days catching the nearby waves, Richard toils in his seaside shop, making infusions of pungent fresh ginger for his ganache, pouring chocolate into molds for cardamom-flavored bars, and cajoling flavor from black tea and seductive spices for his elegant assortment of chocolates. Don't let the breezy beachside attitude fool you. Richard Donnelly's chocolates are serious contenders in the competitive world of chocolate. When asked why he's in the chocolate business, Richard just pats his stomach. On my visit, he passed me a chocolate filled with runny caramel, lightly salted, which included a crunchy bit of roasted macadamia nut. It was amazing. In spite of his jovial way, this guy means business.

For serious chocolate fans, Richard has a Chocolate of the Month Club. He'll personally mail you a different selection of chocolates each month. Richard also hand molds replicas of a Champagne bottle with dark Belgian Callebaut chocolate and fills them with assorted dipped chocolates or ganache-filled truffles, to your preference. Although he gets incredibly busy the few months before Christmas, he takes the time to wait on the customers himself, his apron smudged with chocolate, handing out chocolates to try while you decide which ones you'll be leaving with. One cannot help but exit with a neatly wrapped package of chocolates tied with a handsome bow. And to make sure your chocolates make it home in perfect condition, they're accompanied with a miniature coolant gel-pack to protect against the blazing heat outside.

Driving out of town, I passed surfers in board shorts heading toward the nearby waves. Bicyclists breezed past along the scenic coastal highway. The sky was blue and sunny. Seagulls swooped overhead, and I realized that the California dream is still alive in cheerful Santa Cruz, an oceanside paradise, captured and enrobed in smooth, dark chocolate.

Richard Donnelly Chocolates

1509 Mission Street
Santa Cruz, California 95060
1-888-685-1871
www.donnellychocolates.com

DOES CHOCOLATE GET ANY FRESHER?

I was totally unprepared when I walked into the back of possibly the most resplendent chocolate shop in the world: the elegant Bernachon boutique in Lyon, the gastronomic capital of France and perhaps the world.

Peering through the front window of the pristine shop are spiky, frilly president cakes, topped with shaved chocolate and hazelnut praline, and with candied cherries hidden within. Once inside the shop, you'll discover the flakiest *pain au chocolat*, pristine *macarons au chocolat* with chocolate ganache sandwiched between them, and stunning cakes with such exotic names as *Aveline,* filled with *gianduja* and rum; *Ardéchois,* with marzipan and chestnut cream; and the elegant *Antillais,* with kirsch cream and candied pineapple enrobed in shiny-smooth chocolate glaze.

In spite of all these gorgeous desserts, the most fascinating thing about Bernachon is the tablets of extraordinary chocolate that they make right behind the boutique. In the back of the very elegant shop there is a very different world, where earthy cacao beans are roasted and ground to a super-smooth paste, then used to create their glamorous chocolate pastries and to fabricate the huge variety of chocolate bars sold right in the shop. There are just a handful of small-scale confectioners in the world that produce their own chocolate, and many of them have trained right here at Bernachon.

Each time I visit, I make sure to pick up a stack of their superb bars of chocolate. *Chocolat Amer* is their most bittersweet, *Kalouga* is full of runny, oozing caramel, perfectly accented with flakes of sea salt, and my favorite, *Moka*—bars formed from a slightly sweetened blend of cacao and coffee beans.

Of course, there are also filled chocolates of so many shapes and varieties—a staggering selection! But the favorite and most famous are the *palets d'or*, soft ganache disks enrobed within bittersweet chocolate, finished with a fleck of gold leaf.

I was lucky enough to tour the entire shop, which is a throwback to another era. Everyone seemed to be going about their task of dipping chocolates, decorating cakes, stirring batters, and spreading chocolate on just about everything in sight. They all seemed to be working with passion (I mean, how could they *not*?). On the kitchen stove, brilliant orange peels were being candied in enormous copper vessels, to be included in *Pavé Orange* chocolates or simply cut into crystallized batons and passed under a cascade of dark chocolate for *L'Orangette*. As I walked by, a worker handed me a *Grenoble*, full of creamy chocolate mousse topped with a walnut half so perfect I didn't want to ruin it. (But I knew I had to...in the name of research.) I loved the fact that the chocolate was possibly made just hours before in the next room, and here I was eating a pristine chocolate that could not have been any fresher.

I continued to the area where the raw cacao beans are measured, roasted, and blended. As many as 11 different beans are part of Bernachon's blend of chocolate. After careful roasting, the chocolate is ground between granite rollers, then tempered and deposited into 2- to 3-kilogram bar molds. When I inquired about the specific weight of each bar, the chocolate maker laughed and said, "This is artisan work. We don't measure in specifics. Only quality."

As I marveled at the grinding, a bin was wheeled by, piled high with a dark, coarse paste. Of course I not-indiscreetly inquired, hoping they'd offer a taste. Sure enough, a spoon was handed to me. I dug in. I had what can only be described as one of the best chocolate experiences I have ever had—a mass of ground cacao beans and roasted coffee beans, rounded out with exactly the right amount of sugar. It was dark, bittersweet, utterly delicious. When I learned it was to be further ground into their *Moka* bars, I knew exactly what I would be returning back home with.

Bernachon is in a class by itself, as evidenced by the steady stream of customers that swarm into the shop all day long—visitors lucky enough to live nearby. Others make the pilgrimage from all around the world to experience "Bernachon Passion." Tasting Bernachon chocolate is a revelation in freshness, an experience not to be missed.

Bernachon

42, Cours Franklin-Roosevelt
69006 Lyon, France
Tel: (33) 4 78 24 37 98 / Fax: (33) 4 78 52 67 77
www.bernachon.com

the great book of chocolate

The Whole World Loves Nutella

The first taste I had of Nutella was during a student sojourn through Europe with a backpack and a thick travel guide during my early 20s. I serendipitously hopped trains and hitchhiked from youth hostels to campgrounds, seeking out inexpensive but delicious things to eat along the way to keep me going. It was then I found myself scraping clean my first jar of Nutella. I remember thinking, "This stuff is great. Chocolate for breakfast! I'm going to start every day with this for the rest of my life." However, I could only carry just a few precious jars back with me, and my torrid affair with Nutella, like the rest of that trip, became just a hazy memory.

Hazelnut and chocolate spread originated in Alba, Italy, during World War II, in the 1940s. Because chocolate was rationed, pastry maker Pietro Ferrero blended cocoa powder, cocoa butter, oil, and toasted hazelnuts into a delicious spread. Within a few years, school children lined up for "The Smearing" at local shops, where a slice of bread from home would be smeared with what was then called *Supercrema Gianduja*.

By 1964, the popularity of this chocolate and hazelnut spread had traveled throughout Europe. The spread was introduced outside of Italy and renamed Nutella, which had more global appeal and was easier to pronounce. Now Nutella is the best-selling spread in Europe and is available all over the world. The recipe has been altered slightly, but each 13-ounce jar contains over 50 hazelnuts. Still family owned, Nutella outsells all brands of peanut butter—combined!

THE MOST EXTRAORDINARY CHOCOLATE SHOP IN BELGIUM

In Brussels, chocolate practically overflows into the streets from the overload of chocolate shops. There are literally several chocolate shops on every block. Normally, this would make finding the best quite a grueling task. However, I lucked out my very first try.

I was in Wieze, near Brussels, attending chocolate school at Callebaut College. On a day off from classes, I set off on foot to discover Brussels. I began my journey in the chic place du Grand Sablon, knowing nothing about a special chocolate place I would happen to encounter. As I walked by, I marveled at the gleaming showcases with rows and rows of chocolates lined up. I went inside, a bit intimidated, until the genial woman behind the counter inquired if I'd like her to assemble an order. While I pondered the chocolates in the front showcase, what happened next became a pivotal moment in my life. I needed a few more in my box to fill it properly. As I stood in a sea of indecision, she raised a tasteful eyebrow and said, *"Avec crème fraîche, monsieur?"*

She led me to the rear of the shop. Discreetly stacked on the counter were a few open boxes of chocolate, looking quite innocent, with names like *Café*, *Pistache*, and *Grand Marnier*. I thought "Why not?" and asked her to include a few in my assortment. As I walked out into the *Sablon*, I opened the box and bit into the coffee-flavored chocolate.

I stopped. I was stunned. I took another bite.

The second bite was better than the first. Imagine biting into the thinnest layer of dark chocolate. Enclosed within that crispy, chocolatey layer, a creamy, airy, yet dense filling of whipped *crème fraîche* exploded in my mouth. I was swooning.

Since 1910, the Wittamer family has been making chocolates in the place du Grand Sablon, which has since become the most fashionable square in Belgium. Wittamer is still family run and each of their chocolates is still made by hand. They are the standard of Belgian chocolates that all others aspire to. Paul Wittamer recommends that you eat most of their chocolates within the week they are made. Because they are so utterly fresh they will not last much longer. I love the *Cardinal*, rich with pistachio paste; *Carioca,* with coffee cream (imagine a rich mocha, lightly whipped, enclosed in a thin shell of bittersweet chocolate); and the grand *Bouchon*, heaped with a mound of Grand Marnier cream over a caramelized almond.

Wittamer Chocolate

6, 12-13 Place du Grand Sablon
1000 Brussels, Belgium
Tel: (32) 2 512 37 42 / Fax: (32) 2 512 52 09
www.wittamer.com

A Week in a Chocolate Shop

My fantasy has always been to spend a week playing in the best chocolate shop in the world. My dream came true when Wittamer allowed me the uncommon opportunity to spend time dipping and enrobing in their venerable boutique during the hectic week before Christmas. It was an experience I will never forget. By the end of the week, I was terribly sad to bid farewell to all the fine chocolates, and the lovely people who craft them, within the world of Wittamer.

DAY #1: TUESDAY

For breakfast I have Special K cereal with chocolate chips. (Only in Belgium would a health-promoting cereal have chocolate chips.) I enter the workshop by 8 AM and Wittamer is already a frenzy of activity. As I walk a bit dazed through the kitchen and various workshops, I see bakers piping chocolate mousse into cake molds at blazing speeds. At another table, women in starched white blouses are carefully filling shiny pink Wittamer boxes with chocolates. And all throughout, Paul Wittamer is racing around overseeing everything, clipboard in hand, monitoring the work being done. His sister Myriam breezes past, rushing about looking oh-so-stylish, overseeing the jewel-like boutique and making sure that each box that leaves Wittamer is picture-perfect.

It's time to work. I'm led to the lower level, the chocolate workshop where I will be working during this very busy, incredibly hectic week before Christmas, the most stressful time of the year. In the chocolate workshop, among all the commotion and activity, the room is filled with sounds of clacking and scraping as chocolate is quickly poured and scraped clean from hard plastic *plaques* (molds). Along the wall, the humming enrober carries chocolates down the conveyer belt through a glossy downpour of chocolate. My eyes spot a single cream-filled chocolate on the counter, cracked open, spilling its creamy center onto the countertop. Obviously it's a mistake; I resist the urge to pop it into my mouth.

I am put right to work. My first task is to coat hazelnut praline slabs with a thin layer of chocolate using a paint gun, Wittamer's special method for achieving a distinctly thin chocolate coating. Within moments of being sprayed, the chocolate cools and I cut the slabs into neat, bite-sized rectangles. Off to the side I notice an errant bowl of odd-sized chocolate praline slab end-bits, which I assume are there for me to nibble on. There's always going to be a certain amount of waste, and I am more than willing to take care of as much as I can for them.

Almost as soon as I finish wiping telltale signs of chocolate off my lips, the just-coated hazelnut praline pieces are quickly cut and placed on the conveyer belt to enter the dark chocolate enrobing machine. "Wow, that

was fast!" I think. As they pass through the enrober, someone positioned where they emerge scribbles each with an elegant cursive of milk chocolate. The moment they're firm, they are neatly arranged in little trays and rushed to the chocolate shop, just steps away, ready to be sold. I'm amazed at the speed and precision with which we made them. I was right; this would be quite an experience.

During the afternoon, I'm put to work artfully arranging various chocolates of different sizes, shapes, and textures in 500-gram (about 1-pound) boxes. This is an art form unto itself. Wearing gloves to protect the chocolates from fingerprints, I nestle each chocolate *praline* (the Belgian word for a filled or enrobed chocolate) perfectly against the others in the pink Wittamer boxes. Chocolates that have cracks, chips, scratches, or any other flaws are put into a box marked *pas jolie* (not pretty). This would become the source of my snacking for the week. I learn that it takes hours to fill just 25 boxes by hand. Each chocolate is placed in just the proper spot and handled delicately to ensure that they arrive in perfect condition so that the recipient is enthralled by the chocolates within.

DAY #2: WEDNESDAY

I arrive at 9 AM: the staff has been buzzing in the workshop since 6 AM. This is the week before Christmas, and things are really in full swing. Touy, who has worked at Wittamer for over 20 years (I began to call him *Professeur* Touy for teaching me so much) is enrobing domed mounds of white chocolate ganache studded with roasted almonds and pistachios, called *Rochers Blanc*. Blissfully, Touy has developed a habit of passing to me whatever chocolate he happens to be dipping. We're busy, but that *Rochers Blanc* was absolutely the best white chocolate confection I have ever eaten and it keeps me fueled for the next few hours.

No sooner have I savored the last bite than I am put to work scraping excess chocolate from stacks of polycarbonate *plaques*, preparing them to be filled with smooth dark chocolate ganache. Chocolate that we remove from the plaques is returned to the tempering kettle, which contains the chocolate used to coat, fill, and enrobe each and every chocolate at Wittamer. I pondered whether my home kitchen could be fitted with a similar tempering kettle.

By the afternoon, I am summoned to the packaging room, where I wrap chocolates for the shop. The boutique is running dangerously low and the crowds are scooping up as many boxes as they can for Christmas. We don't want any riots. Today I time myself. I fill 40 boxes, each with 35 chocolates, and it takes me almost $2^1/_2$ hours to fill all of the boxes. Doing the math, it occurs to me that a box of hand-wrapped Wittamer chocolates is perhaps the best bargain in the world.

As I fill boxes, the jovial chef Michael Lewis-Anderson comes by to offer me a chocolate. When I tell him that I've already had way too many, he responds "Oh? How many have you had?" I reply, "About eight." "Eight! Is that all? That's *nothing*! " he laughs.

DAY #3: THURSDAY

I am able to go for a full hour this morning without having any chocolate. After that, I feel it is no longer prudent to resist. I extract a chocolate from the *pas jolie* box, and gingerly bite into *The* (tea), which fills my mouth with an intoxicating blend of citrusy Earl Grey tea and dark chocolate. Okay, I'd better have another I reason unreasonably, so I follow it with *Pâte Feuilletine*, the thinnest square of buttery, crisp, caramelized nut paste coated with just the right amount of shiny dark chocolate.

I peer into the boutique. There's a solid line of customers. Myriam Wittamer alerts us that they're seriously low on prepacked boxes of chocolate, having gone through all the boxes we had spent the previous day meticulously assembling. I spend the next nine hours packing boxes, swanky pink mini-hatboxes and larger, grander *ballotins*. I am amazed at how much care is required to complete each box. But I figure since a customer might just eat 1 chocolate and judge the quality of Wittamer based on that bite, I know to take extra care to make sure each perfect chocolate is packed in the box just right.

While packing chocolates and chatting with chef Michael, I learn that Paul Wittamer actually eats several of his favorite chocolates each day. His favorite, I find out, is *Tarragone*, two interlocking milk chocolate hearts filled with a superb dense filling of ground Italian hazelnut paste. ("Hmm, I'd better try that one of those too...")

I am amazed at the freshness of the chocolates the boutique sells. Saleswomen actually hurry all day between the boutique and the chocolate workshop to snatch chocolates, barely cooled, right off the conveyer belt of the enrober.

By the end of today, I am a bit weary, probably from the combination of standing all day and not eating quite enough chocolate. My aching body is relieved at dinner at my favorite local restaurant, *Aux Vieux Bruxelles*, where I and some Wittamer staff "debrief" over *Moules-Frites*— and perhaps a few too many goblets of Chimay Belgian beer. I can't remember.

DAY #4: FRIDAY

Today I eat only 3 chocolates.

I had a dream the previous night about a giant jar of Nutella pursuing me through some weird passageways. I was tired. I think I slept in some of my work clothes. I woke up smelling faintly of chocolate and probably a touch of beer.

Back in the shop, I arrive and the staff is working at full tilt. I'm immediately recruited to scoop dark liquid chocolate from the tempering machine into chocolate *plaques* that resemble corncobs, to make a praline called *Maize*. Once the chocolate is firm in the molds, we pipe in a runny nut paste with tiny bits of chocolate. The filling is soft so I need to pipe fast. Really fast. The creamy filling is quickly oozing from the pastry tip slightly faster than I can move. I fill each chocolate-lined corn-shaped mold over the rim, then deftly scrape the excess filling from the *plaques* and rapidly slap 2 together to enclose the runny filling, to be unmolded later once the chocolate has set. We fill hundreds and hundreds of these *plaques*.

Afterward we fill several hundred milk chocolate–lined heart-shaped *plaques* with a darker, similarly nutty paste. My arms are splattered with chocolate well above my elbows and my hair and face are coated with a thin layer of cocoa butter. All this cocoa butter must be very good for my skin, I hope.

At lunchtime, I peek into the chocolate boutique, where patrons are packed in, waiting to pick up their Christmas orders. The biggest gift available at Wittamer comes in an enormous shiny pink box, aptly named *Hercule* (Hercules). It's huge, and brimming with fabulous Wittamer chocolates, delicate rose petal jelly, chocolate *mendiats* studded with candied fruits and nuts, house-made *pâte de fruit* (fruit jellies), and a bottle of their insignia champagne. The saleswomen are in a frenzy, patiently listening to customers, packing up orders, and securing them with big lacy bows. The packing room of the boutique is a mad riot of ribbon snippets, boxes, wrapping paper, decorative paper, and, of course, chocolate.

In the chocolate workshop, the chocolatiers are unwrapping big blocks of Callebaut "Origin Select" chocolate. I snatch a taste as the chocolate is melted into a smooth ganache along with some cream. Before we leave, all the countertops in the vast kitchens are scrupulously cleaned then lined with heavy plastic wrap. The warm chocolate paste is spread thickly over every inch of the plastic-lined countertops to cool overnight. As I pack up my bags to leave, I sneak a taste. Excellent! The one I taste combines intense bittersweet dark chocolate with the bright flavor of fresh ginger.

Outside, light, wispy snowflakes are falling. I'm in Belgium and I can't resist a snack as I head home and pass a sidewalk vendor grilling thick, eggy Belgian waffles coated with a smear of chocolate. I have one. It's really good and I think to myself, "Is there really anything more perfect right now, in this moment, than a warm waffle coated with Belgian chocolate?"

DAY #5: SATURDAY

I arrive a bit late and the staff is in full swing. Oops.

The filling for their famous *crème fraîche* chocolates had been made and whipped already. The place is alive with energy. Chocolatiers pile the buttery and terrifically rich filling into thin chocolate shells. A few delicate shells break every now and then, so I assume eating a few is another way I can help out. While we're in the midst of the filling frenzy, a woman from the boutique comes running through, speaking excitedly in French. The entire workshop comes to a screeching halt and we scramble to rapidly pack a few boxes of just-made chocolates and rush them into the boutique. She comes back a few minutes later. She needs more!

My day continues as I work in tandem alongside another chocolatier. Working together, we spray the thinnest layer of chocolate onto square slabs of ganache, then cut the slabs into neat squares using dueling "guitars." Each guitar is actually a series of parallel wires that cuts the slabs into long, perfectly even strips. The entire slab is rotated a quarter turn and cut again, creating about 100 perfect squares, which are immediately fed into the enrobing machine As they emerge, still wet, a sturdy design-embossed sheet is gently pressed into the warm chocolate. As they firm up, the design sheets made of cocoa butter will be lifted off, and a crisp design will remain, beautifully impressed in each chocolate.

An older, diminutive woman works alongside me as we cut slabs of ganache. I notice that she's effortlessly slicing twice as many slabs as I am. She's lifting the weighty slabs, transferring them to the guitar, lowering the heavy slicing panel with the cutting wires, stacking the chocolate squares, then hefting the stacks onto a rack. I'm impressed and a bit humbled.

After a much-appreciated lunch break, I set about removing the cocoa-butter patterned sheets on the chocolates that we made earlier. As I remove each sheet, every time I think "Oh my, these are beautiful." Afterward, each chocolate is placed by hand into boxes for the boutique. Just for the record, I count 16 boxes that I pack up. Each box contains 175 chocolate—2,800 chocolates in all! And they will shortly be gone, sent to the boutique and out the door.

As we near the end of the day, we scrape excess chocolate from the *plaques* we use to make filled chocolates. These *plaques* have really had a workout this week. Each mold gets used over and over to create chocolates. Each day is spent smearing tempered chocolate up to the rims into each *plaque*, then scraping away excess chocolate. The *plaques* get inverted over the tempering kettle and vibrated to remove air bubbles and excess chocolate. Afterward more chocolate is scraped away. Filling is added, then the *plaques* are briefly chilled. Finally, a last layer of chocolate is spread across the bottom to create a seal. Once again, excess chocolate is cleanly scraped away. They're chilled briefly, then the chocolate pralines are released from the *plaques* and everyone scrambles to pack the chocolates neatly into boxes, wearing gloves for hygiene and to prevent fingerprints from marring the perfect chocolate coating.

We end this very long day by scrubbing every surface of the chocolate workshop clean with very hot water, wiping away chocolate that's been flung and sprayed, dripped and dipped.

DAY #6: SUNDAY

Okay, the home stretch.

Only 2 days before Christmas. Although we've been working hard the entire week before, today we're all especially exhausted and punchy. *"Je suis fatigue!"* ("I am tired!") is overheard throughout the kitchens. In fact, many times we catch ourselves doing something a bit loopy; sealing a *plaque* of dark chocolates with milk chocolate by accident, or cutting a slab of ganache that's still attached to the hard plastic underneath. In the adjacent bakery, most of the staff arrived at 2 AM to finish the tremendous amount of orders for chocolate-glazed *Bûche du Nöel*, a traditional European Christmas cake.

I spend most of the day filling *plaques* with dark chocolate. I stand over the tempering kettle, with a stack of *plaques* stacked precariously high to the side. Off I go, quickly overloading each with chocolate then methodically scraping the excess away. I overturn each *plaque* over the tempering machine, which shakes loose extra chocolate and leaves a nice, thin layer. After I pour the chocolate back into the kettle, I scrape again. Then on to the next one. Then the next. I do this for about 2 hours, nonstop, and I realize that I've gotten pretty good at it. But halfway through, my hands get tired and begin cramping. And why is it that every time I get my hands immersed in chocolate, I get a persistent itch on my face?

Today I've come to a conclusion about a question that has been plaguing me all week: which is my favorite chocolate at Wittamer—the cream-filled, buttery chocolates flavored with strong coffee, or the dark chocolate rectangles of ganache with the contrasting tang of passion fruit? At the beginning of the week, my favorite was definitely *Irish Coffee*, a cube of dark chocolate ganache with a sip of whisky enclosing a candied coffee bean and coated with a triple swirl of chocolate. But I also discovered *Poivre*, a simple ganache with a grind of spicy black pepper, giving the chocolate a nice kick. I've decided I like that one best. At least for today.

DAY #7: MONDAY (THE DAY BEFORE CHRISTMAS)

My final day begins with hand dipping a tray of *Bouche Lait*, mini-cylinders of milk chocolate filled with vanilla-scented whipped cream hiding a candied almond. Dipping this delicate confection properly takes me a few tries, but then I get the rhythm going. Although some turn out funny looking, I remember that these are handmade chocolates. They are individual creations, not something that rolls perfectly off an assembly line. Still, I try to improve my technique with each dip, striving toward perfection. Indeed, throughout the week I've learned an incredible amount making so many chocolates in such a short time. We've made about 180 pounds (82 kg) of chocolates by hand in the workshop each day.

As I worked during the week, I learned exactly how firmly to rap the *plaques* to release the chocolates—just enough so they gently fall out, but not too much so they

tumble over each other and scratch or crack. I've learned how to hold the *plaques* just right so that I am able to scrape off precisely the right amount of chocolate. And most important, I made an entire batch of chocolates myself, *Tête de Cheval*, a traditional Belgian horse head design filled with dark hazelnut paste and chocolate filling. I've made them from start to finish. And they look pretty darn good, I think, as I pack them snugly into shiny pink boxes for the boutique.

We finished the day making *Pyramides*. Each bite-size pyramid is a coating of raspberry-flavored white chocolate surrounding a creamy dark chocolate center. We use separate equipment to mix and coat using the vivid, wildly colored pink coating. We work with a mini-enrober, a countertop apparatus that blends the chocolate and dried raspberries into the glossy couverture used to coat each pyramid. What a fitting way to end the week, as we all work together to coat, fill, then seal each *Pyramid*, the signature chocolate praline from Wittamer.

My week at Wittamer gave me a wondrous opportunity to see firsthand the care and attention that distinguishes Belgium's finest chocolate shop. I still get a thrill wandering into their smart Brussels boutique, peering into showcases filled with all sorts of divine chocolate bonbons, awed by the knowledge and skill of the fine artisans at Wittamer, the quintessential expression of Belgian chocolate.

CHOCOLATE IN PARADISE

If you're anything like me, you think about chocolate at home, at work, and even when you're on vacation. In the paradise of the Hawaiian Islands, chef Philippe Padovani creates some unusually delicious chocolates using Hawaiian Vintage Chocolate, grown on Oahu. His fillings include a breezy, creamy mint; a very fruity, tropical Tahitian vanilla caramel; and *Ka'u* orange, which is the essence of the sweet citrus itself.

Padovani Chocolate Boutique

McInerny Galleria
Royal Hawaiian Shopping Center
2301 Kalakaua Avenue
Honolulu, Hawaii 96815
1-808-971-4207

Padovani Restaurant & Wine Bar

1956 Ala Moana Boulevard
Honolulu, Hawaii 96815
1-808-946-3456
www.padovani-e-gourmet.com

SEX SELLS...CHOCOLATE?

I can't think of chocolate more unabashedly sexy than Vosges Haut-Chocolat. Wedged in between the proudly soaring skyscrapers of Chicago is a tiny Vosges shop with clean white lines. Within the shop, the chocolates are set seductively on mirrored presentation slabs as willowy saleswomen tempt you from behind a counter full of jewel-like chocolates.

While I waited to chat with shop owner Katrina Markoff, I snuck a glance behind the curtain to the employee area and saw 3 large signs—"Flirt! Flirt! *Flirt!*" Vosges Haut-Chocolat certainly has no intention of letting anyone leave without being seduced by their personal palette of chocolate flavors, textures, and taste sensations.

Katrina Markoff extracts inspiration from flavors around the world. While often a cliché, Vosges Haut-Chocolat is one place where the unusual is actually more-than-brilliantly realized. Katrina has traveled the globe and worked with some of the most creative chocolatiers and pastry chefs in the world, including the audacious Ferran Adrià of El Bulli in Spain. These experiences awakened her feel for the exotic flavors that she uses to subtly and not-so-subtly scent her chocolates: evocative smoked Hungarian paprika is showered over a dark chocolate truffle, a blaze of curry powder is paired with coconut cream in another truffle, and stimulating fennel pollen from Tuscany elicits a passionate sensation from yet another one of her exotic chocolate truffles.

Visiting her smart, fashionable, and friendly boutique in Chicago or in Soho in New York City, try one of the "haut chocolates," a sensuous on-site tasting of combinations of hot, cold, spicy, sweet, herbal, and roasty. The *Bianca*, a white chocolate fantasy accented with lavender and Australian citrusy myrtle,

Katrina Markoff with her *boîte á Chapeau*

Ten Reasons Chocolate Is Better Than Sex

1. You are never too young or old for chocolate.

2. Good chocolate is easy to find.

3. You can ask a stranger for chocolate without getting your face slapped.

4. The word "commitment" doesn't scare off chocolate.

5. You can make chocolate last as long as you want it to.

6. You can safely have chocolate while driving.

7. When you have chocolate, it doesn't keep your neighbors awake.

8. You can have chocolate even in front of your mother.

9. You can have as many different kinds of chocolate as you can handle.

10. You can have chocolate at work without upsetting your coworkers.

or *Cappuccino une bombe surprise*, a tall, slender intense coffee drink with a truffle dropped into it. (I daringly chose the horseradish-wasabi truffle *bombe*.) But my favorite is the hot *Aztec Elixir*, a spicy, rich cup of dark chocolate blended with cinnamon-like cassia, chipotle, and ancho chiles. Although I strongly recommend trying them in the shop for the entire "Haut-Chocolat" experience, all hot chocolate drink blends are available to whip up at home.

The plushness of the experience is echoed in the packaging, making a gift from Vosges an elegant surprise. Lush purple is the theme, reminiscent of the 1970s colors of vintage Emilio Pucci, in contrast with the clean lines of Katrina's perfectly round dark and milk chocolate truffles. Why not surprise someone who loves chocolate with her *boîte á Chapeau*, a giant hatbox brimming with all sorts of chocolate treats. Or when in Chicago, give yourself the gift of a tasting for all 5 of your senses at the boutique. Before I left, I was presented with a personalized tray of chocolates hand selected especially for me. I began with a taste of golden bee pollen, followed by a squirty whole kumquat, then a blast of intense espresso, a nibble of a curry and coconut milk chocolate truffle, and finally a few salty corn nuts. It was definitely better than, uh...

Vosges Haut-Chocolat

The Shops at Northpoint (520 North Michigan Avenue)
Chicago, Illinois 60611
1-888-301-9866

———

132 Spring Street
New York, New York 10012
www.vosgeschocolate.com

A HUMANITARIAN VISION
OF CHOCOLATE

Most people send a check once in a while to help others, but Steven Wallace actually does it all the time. With chocolate.

Steven Wallace started out on his lifepath when he was just a wide-eyed teenager who had left home for a foreign-exchange experience. When he arrived in Ghana, he found himself living in a home with 1 father, 3 wives, and 21 children! The longer he stayed, the more Steven grew to love the people, the land, and the culture of Ghana.

Later, after he returned to the United States, he remained profoundly affected by his experience in Africa and thought that perhaps the people who grow the cacao beans for chocolate in Ghana should share some of the economic benefits from the sale of the finished product. So in 1991, he opened a chocolate factory in Ghana, where the cacao is actually grown, aiming to create a sustainable business for the Africans. His hope was to use the chocolate to provide a solid economic base for the natives.

Omanhene dark milk chocolate is the result of this undertaking. Steven says he invented "dark" milk chocolate because many people prefer milk chocolate or are just more familiar with it and he wanted to produce a quality chocolate that would appeal to a greater audience. Omanhene dark milk chocolate has more cacao mass than many dark bitter-sweet or semisweet chocolates available, along with the smooth, creamy taste of milk chocolate that most chocolate lovers find comforting. And the colorful, African tribal packaging is possibly the most vivid and stunning of all the chocolate wrappers that I've come across.

Steven believes that, as with other foods, we should think about where our chocolate comes from, shopping and eating in a socially responsible manner even when it comes to chocolate. Omanhene is mostly made from hybrid beans, with varieties that have been raised to be both flavorful and productive. Steven attests to the difficulty of setting up a business in Ghana, but he speaks so passionately about what he's doing that you can't help getting hooked. His mission and his chocolate are important contributions to the chocolate world. So when you eat Omanhene chocolate you can feel like you're doing something not just for yourself, but also for those who make it.

The Omanhene Cocoa Bean Company
www.omanhene.com
1-800-LUV-CHOC

Quick! What's the most sophisticated chocolate bar in the world? If you've just had a Fran's Gold Bar, you'd know the answer. Fran's famous Gold Bars are chocolate-enrobed toasted nuts—almonds or macadamia nuts—layered among buttery-smooth caramel. All of this is as valuable as a gold ingot, and wrapped to resemble one too!

Fran's chocolates, made in the city of Seattle, have been a favorite for more than 30 years. Perhaps the Seattlites who favor Fran's chocolates for fending off the drizzle-induced blues know something that scientists are just learning: chocolate contains a substance that lifts your spirits, similar to the chemical found in many antidepressants. But no matter the reason, you'll be just as happy (and slightly overwhelmed with indecision) when you walk into Fran's retail shop in the University Village district of Seattle. At Easter, there are lavender foil–wrapped Easter eggs, in the autumn there are chocolates filled with Cabernet and Chardonnay grape syrups, and year-round you can experience the ultimate marriage of mint and chocolate in her Cookie Fixations, wide disks of minted chocolate wafer cookies with a white chocolate layer and an extra wham of chocolate via a dark chocolate coating.

Just about all of Fran's chocolates are made in her Bellevue workshop from Venezuelan *criollo* chocolate, noted for its intense fruity characteristics. Chocolatiers in her workshops work diligently, hand wrapping holiday treats, carefully buffing the foil on each piece by hand to a lustrous sheen. A well-worn copper kettle bubbles on the stove, with Fran checking the temperature as she passes, focusing on getting the caramel filling to the right stage of rich darkness. But what impresses me the most is Fran's quiet diligence, going from worker to worker, from table to table, checking on progress, assisting as necessary, and overseeing everything in her busy workshop, which chocolate experts universally agree provides some of the best chocolates in America.

I recruited my friend Carla Duncan, a die-hard chocolate fan (who has a dedicated chocolate cellar in her basement) to come along on my visit to Fran's retail shop. A local expert, Carla immediately steered me toward the freezer, where a young man was earnestly scooping ice cream. Of course, I had to try the chocolate ice cream, which was accompanied with a scoop of burnt turbinado sugar ice cream. The bittersweet chocolate flavor was an absolutely delightful counterpoint to the burnt-sweet caramelized ice cream. Managing to divert herself from the chocolate for a brief respite, Carla assured me the lemon ice cream was like eating a wedge of tangy lemon meringue pie. She was right!

But for chocolate lovers like us, the ice cream was only an introduction—we wanted more! Fueled by good Seattle-style espresso and hot cocoa topped with whipped cream and freshly shaved chocolate, we crossed forks in Fran's crumbly, moist chocolate torte. *Food & Wine* called it one of the great chocolate cakes of the world. We agreed. The cake resembled a dense chocolate mousse and had the three characteristics I like best in a chocolate mousse: richness, richness, and more richness.

Before our reluctant departure, I scanned the offerings of dipped chocolates neatly displayed in perfect rows in the best European tradition. I walked away with a ribbon-wrapped box heavy with caramels accented with a few flakes of French sea salt, spheres of ganache-filled truffles, and Nibbits, tiny chocolate-crusted cacao nibs.

Fran's Chocolates

2504 NE University Village
Seattle, Washington 98105
1-800-422-3726
www.franschocolates.com

THEY'RE NUMBER ONE!

What does *Consumer Reports* know about chocolate? Well, plenty, it seems. When they tested chocolates for a Valentine's issue, Martine's Chocolates came out in first place, heads above a very distinguished group of chocolates. After reading this, I immediately rang Martine's and requested a mixed box of chocolates. Unfortunately, it was summer and owner Martine Penechek refuses to sell chocolates unless she can guarantee they will arrive in perfect condition. So I had to wait for a break in the summertime heat of New York City. Just when I almost forgot about ever getting even a morsel of Martine's Chocolates, I picked up the phone one day and it was Martine excitedly telling me about a break in the heat wave, otherwise know as "summer in New York City," allowing her to rush a box across the country to me. My chocolate was on the way!

Thankfully the box of chocolates arrived safely. Inside was the handwritten note, "Please eat within 5 days of purchase," which they include in every box they ship. On the accompanying guide, there was a printed message stating that what I was about to eat were "pieces (of chocolate)...made with fresh cream" along with more admonitions about storing them correctly and enjoying them as soon as possible, with the last circled twice for emphasis! Not a problem in my house.

When the announcement that Martine's Chocolates were the best in the United States was published, Martine was swamped with orders, showing just how excited people were to discover great chocolate. Speaking to her, you can hear the excitement as she talks about her chocolates. You'll be just as enthused about chocolate after you untie the bow on the glossy, electric-pink *ballotin* of Martine's Chocolates.

I challenge you to decide which to eat first. A handy guide is provided that designates just how each chocolate is filled. My favorite was Cherry, a dark chocolate dome enclosing a candied sour cherry marinated in brandy atop a layer of soft chocolate ganache. Heart was a big surprise. The guide said it was cappuccino, which sounds innocent but turns out to have the strength of dark Italian espresso with a dollop of cream. Tall, imposing Pyramid had a whipped cream filling studded with ground roasted hazelnuts bound together with caramel, and Three Hills was a triple-whammy blend of her best Belgian chocolates all in a single bonbon. All of Martine's chocolates use a unique blend of Callebaut chocolate, which she imports especially from Belgium.

So next time you're near Bloomingdales in New York City, where Martine's Chocolates are created, take a chocolate break and watch Martine and her chocolatiers craft individual pieces of chocolate filled with the freshest whipping cream. Or, have Martine send you some, so you can judge for yourself—just don't place your order in summer!

Martine's Chocolates

6th Floor, Blomingdale's
1000 Third Avenue
New York, New York 10022-1231
1-212-705-2347
www.martineschocolates.com

Thank goodness there's such a fantastic variety of chocolates to choose from. From dark, bittersweet blocks of artisan chocolate for nibbling to smooth ganache-filled creamy candies to savor on special occasions, there seems to be something new to discover all the time. A younger generation of chocolate makers constantly tempts us with ambitious creations, and yet the classic chocolatiers continue to dazzle us with elegant confections. What more could a chocophile want?

La Chataigne

2,60 €

Chocolate in Paris

It seems as though every conversation in Paris becomes a gastronomic tête-à-tête. I've had many lively discussions with Parisians regarding who makes the best chocolates, where the best places are to get them, and even what the best way is to enjoy them! So it's no coincidence that no other city in the world seems to have as many fantastic chocolate boutiques as Paris. Chocolate lovers from all over the world make pilgrimages to Paris because it's saturated with chocolate—in tea salons, crepe vendors, department stores, chocolate boutiques, pâtisseries, confectionery kiosks, boulangeries, and epiceries. Each quarter has a special address where you can discover some of the finest chocolates found anywhere in the world. In the following pages are many of my favorite places—should you be lucky enough to make a visit to this magical city with more chocolate shops than you can possibly imagine. Note that some of these shops have several locations. In those cases, I've listed the main shop, but if a web address is given, check for additional locations.

A STITCH IN TIME

Reported to be the oldest confectionery shop in Paris, you'll be charmed immediately as you pass though the doorway, away from the bustle of the Montmarte. Check the lovely window display of chocolate mendiants decorated with skinned hazelnuts, candied orange, and brilliant green Sicilian pistachios. Founded in 1761, A La Mére de Famille retains that age-old Parisian feeling with glass showcases and gilded antique labels decorating just about every surface. Select among tablets of chocolate, huge florentines swirled with dark or milk chocolate, candied roasted almonds tumbled in chocolate and dusted with cocoa, or *çalissons d'Aix* (diamond-shaped, moist, almond-rich Provençal confections).

A La Mére de Famille

35, Faubourg Montmarte, 9th
Métro: Grand Boulevards
01.47.70.83.69

WELCOME TO HER WORLD

The sign on the door should read "Beware of flying pigtails." Instead a doorway clustered with vintage chocolate posters and memorabilia marks the entrance into the world of Denise Acabo, who delivers the most fabulous chocolate shopping experience around. Show the slightest interest in chocolate and Madame Acabo tells you about all the different and sensational chocolates that she sells. Sporting girlish pigtails, Madame Acabo dances through her shop in a crisp pleated skirt, buzzing with enthusiasm. She's the proverbial kid in her own candy store.

The famed Bernachon chocolates (page 56) are available here. She is the only one they trust outside their shop in Lyon

 to sell their chocolate bars and chocolates. She also sells the hard-to-find handmade chocolate from Pralus and Bernard Dufoux (page 154), plus my favorite caramels in the world, C.B.S. (caramel, butter, and salt) from Le Roux chocolatier (page 155) in Brittany. Although chocolatiers from all over France try to sway her with samples, hoping to make it into her shop, Denise is not easily impressed and has no trouble telling chocolatiers why their chocolates are not good enough for her and her customers.

The (Chocolate) Lovers of Paris

Parisians are so fanatical about quality of chocolate, there is a society of chocolate tasters, Club des Croqueurs de Chocolat, which meets frequently to discuss and taste chocolate. This ultra-exclusive society limits membership to 150 members and naturally has a very long waiting list (I believe I am somewhere around 7,630). New members are carefully screened and must be "sponsored" by 2 current members.

But you don't need to be a member to spy on the results of their chocolate tastings. Log on to their website at www.webender.com/croqueurs, where chocolate shops and their wares are ranked with 1 to 5 chocolate bars, signifying the results of the group's tastings.

Paris also hosts an annual Salon du Chocolat, often the final weekend of October. Many of the major chocolatiers and chocolate manufacturers set up huge displays and hand out samples to eager Parisians. The usually reserved Parisians forget all their manners as they jostle for positions at the demonstrations and dispensing of chocolate samples. More subdued Salon du Chocolat events take place once a year in New York City and in Luxembourg. Due to the popularity of chocolate, they are considering other cities to host other salons around the world. Visit www.chocoland.com for dates and locations.

When I offered to bring her some of my homemade Rocky Road (page 144), she told me, "I don't allow chocolate and peanuts together in my shop."

Denise's enthusiasm makes the place seem like a wacky dream brought on by eating maybe a bit too much chocolate. The antidote, of course, is an Anti-Stress Bar, made by Bernard Dufoux, a mélange of soft chocolate and crispy nuts, along with nubbins of dried and candied fruits. If you plan to visit, give yourself plenty of extra time, as you'll find yourself enthralled and charmed by this French woman's fantasy world.

A l'Etoile d'Or

30, rue Fontaine, 9th
Métro: Blanche
01.48.74.59.55

WORLD'S BEST CHOCOLATE ICE CREAM

You may think that you have had great chocolate ice cream, but after you visit Berthillon, you'll forget all the ice creams you've ever had. Creamy, dark, rich, intense, and bittersweet all come to mind as you walk away lapping at your *cornet* (cone) of *chocolat amer* (bitter chocolate) from the street-front window. You'll have plenty of time to decide which flavor to choose while you wait, but once it's your turn, you'd better know what you want! On my last visit there were four different varieties of chocolate ice cream. If you can't make it to the shop (or if you visit in sweltering August, when most of Paris, and Berthillon, takes a holiday) you'll find Berthillon ice creams and sorbets in many nearby cafes on the Ile St.-Louis and across Paris—just look for signs designating Glace Berthillon.

Berthillon

31, rue Saint-Louis d'Ile, 4th
Métro: Pont Marie
01.43.54.31.61

A WORLD OF CHOCOLATE

La Grand Epiceries of Paris at the Bon Marché department store take up an entire block on the Left Bank and I can't imagine a more grand place to do your grocery shopping. There is a selection of chocolates from around the globe, but especially well represented are French chocolate makers Michel Cluizel, Bonnat, and Weiss. The Bon Marché is the perfect place to stock up on blocks of chocolates for chocolate comparison. Try the tasting kit from Michel Cluizel, which allows you to compare chocolates from seven regions of the world.

La Grand Epicerie / Le Bon Marché

22, rue de Sèvres, 7th
Métro: Sévres-Babylone
01.44.39.81.00

the great book of chocolate

CUP OF CACAO?

Follow the beckoning swags of cacao vines hanging at the door and inside you'll find a modern array of beautiful chocolates. Try a square of creamy *gianduja* with hazelnuts or a knob of enrobed ganache with crisped rice inside—so very *au courant* in Paris. Comfy chairs provide a place for those who want to rest and sip hot chocolate in the winter, served from a polished copper chocolate urn. Be sure to visit Paris's oldest bakery, Stohrer, just up the way, at 51, rue Montorgueil.

Charles Chocolatier

15, rue Montorgeuil, 2nd
Métro: Les Halles or Etienne Marcel
01.45.08.57.77

HAVE YOUR CAKE

Come here for the glossy slick-as-ice *tarte au chocolat* with a rich chocolate crust—one of my favorite French chocolate experiences. Other chocolate gâteaux from Christian Constant include *Macao*, delicate chocolate cake layered with a pour of dark Jamaican rum, a bold *Fondant Moka* with Arabica coffee, and the *Soleil Noir*, a dome of pure chocolate ganache scented with Ceylon cinnamon.

The rather brutal chocolate that Constant uses to enrobe his chocolates tends to overwhelm the floral and spice essences he uses to flavor the aromatic fillings, but where else can you sample chocolates flavored with saffron, frangipani, sesame nougat, and ylang ylang?

Christian Constant

37, rue d'Assas, 6th
Métro: Rennes or Saint-Placide
01.53.63.15.15
Christian.constant@wanadoo.fr

THE CHOCOLATE SALON

This gem of a shop is a quiet, sedate place where the most refined (yes, you!) can gently select chocolates. Hold your breath as the saleswomen deftly lift each chocolate ever so nimbly with their silver servers and, with utmost care, place it neatly in the box while you decide on your next selection. What began 2 centuries ago as a partnership between a chocolatier and a pharmacist to dispense chocolate has become the fanciest chocolate salon in Paris.

Should it be the 72% ganache *palet d'or*, or the caramelized almond nougat covering a milk chocolate ganache and covered with sinful dark chocolate? Or would you like to try the chewy nougat de Montelimar enrobed in dark chocolate? Allow the saleswoman to pack your chocolates in neat rows, secure them with a fancy satin ribbon, and send you on your way. Then exhale.

Debauve & Gallais

30, rue des Saints-Pères, 7th
Métro: St. Germain-des Prés
01.45.10.34.67
www.debauve-et-gallais.com

THE ULTIMATE CANDY STORE

Fouquet is one of that few stores in Paris that specializes in candies. I love wandering through the shop, peering into the pricey little jars that hold just a few candies, including chocolate-covered almonds, perfect palets filled with creamy chocolate underneath a slick coating of couverture, chocolate toffee with fleur de sel, and mocha-flavored coffee "beans." During the year, they create molded chocolate containers shaped like giant Easter eggs, clamshells, ducks, or fish that can be filled with candies from the huge glass jars that decorate the shop.

Fouquet

22, rue François 1er,
Métro: FDR
01.47.23.30.36
www.fouquet.fr

BREAKFAST OF CHAMPIONS

My rule is to stop at Gèrard Mulot the morning after I arrive in Paris. I do so because there I can order a very dark *café express* and accompany it with his fabulous chocolate and coconut fondant. At first glance this rich cake appears to be muffinlike, but one bite will make you say au revoir to anything but these ultrarich petit cakes. This is without a doubt one of Paris's most elegant chocolate and pastry shops and should not be missed.

Gèrard Mulot

76, rue de Seine, 6th
Métro: Odéon
01.43.26.85.77

PAIN AU CHOCOLAT EXTRAORDINAIRE

Primarily known for their breads, M. Poujauran's shop is well worth a visit for the extraordinary *pain au chocolat*. Shatteringly crispy, buttery puff pastry wrapped around batons of intense dark chocolate—the perfect start to the day (although it's also a favorite late-afternoon snack of many Parisians).

Jean-Luc Poujauran

20, rue Jean-Nicot, 7th
Métro: La Tour-Maubourg
01.47.05.80.88

OF CHEESE AND CHOCOLATE

The chocolate-dipped figs are luscious. The truffles are sublime. But the cheese-accented chocolates are an experience not to be missed. Huh? Tangy chèvre, Epoisse with cumin, golden Livarot from Normandy, and cave-ripened Roquefort are all used in Jean-Paul Hévin's apéritif chocolate selection. Though I was initially hesitant, the first creamy bite erased my skepticism. The faint sweetness of cheese whipped into a lightly sweetened mousse covered with a very thin chocolate shell was just perfect. Ah, the French. Who else could so successfully combine the cheese course with dessert?

Tablets of chocolate with different cacao percentages are sold; a handy guide will tell you what flavor sensations you should expect. An upstairs tea room serves a multitude of chocolate desserts, as well as a sensational apple tarte Tatin, but most are chocolate, including Pyramid (layers of chocolate génoise with almond paste, pistachios, and bitter chocolate ganache) and Safi (a chocolate almond-enriched génoise spread with dark, rich chocolate mousse embedded with bits of candied orange).

Jean-Paul Hévin

231, rue Fabourg St. Honore, 1st
Métro: Tuilleries
01.55.35.35.96
www.jphevin.com

MACAROON MECCA

Does Ladurée really have the absolutely most fantastic, chewiest *macarons* (macaroons) in the world? Their famous plump biscuits beckon from window displays and are made with a secret recipe known only to their bakers. Their dainty tea room on the rue Royale (or their stunningly renovated Beaux Arts shop at 75, Champs-Elysées) is a favorite place in Paris for a terrific sweet *petit déjeuner* of *pain au chocolat* (chocolate croissants) and a steaming pot of hot chocolate, as well as an amazing assortment of macaroons filled with chocolate, pistachio, lemon, café, caramel...

Ladurée

16, rue Royale, 8th
Métro: Madeleine
01.42.60.21.79
www.laduree.fr

PICTURE OF PERFECTION

Everything is perfect at La Maison du Chocolat. Walk into any one of the chic, friendly boutiques of La Maison du Chocolat, and you'll find yourself immersed in a world where all that matters is chocolate. It's a world filled with perfect confections and pristine presentations, all presented in rich cocoa-brown packaging. You'll find honey and orange flower nougat dipped in chocolate, *Andalouse* flavored with lemon peel (one of my favorite), and if you come during Christmas, you may find sublime domes of chocolate filled with lighter-than-anything chestnut mousse. What is most appealing about La Maison du Chocolat's chocolate is the beauty in simplicity: clean, pure flavored ganaches, simply coated with impossibly thin dark chocolate couverture.

The locations at 52, rue François 1er and at 89, ave Raymond Poincaré will make you a wondrously rich hot chocolate—the best in Paris—in the winter.

La Maison du Chocolat

52, rue François 1er
Métro: FDR or Georges V

_____

89, ave Raymond Poincaré, 16th
Métro: Victor Hugo
01.40.67.77.88
www.lamaisonduchocolat.com

THE GOLD STANDARD

There are 8 Lenôtre boutiques in Paris (and more around the world). Every pastry sold at the Parisian boutiques is made by hand at Lenôtre's outstanding bakery outside of the city. The selections range from their simple yet ultrarich dark chocolate macaroons to the ultimate version of *Gâteau Opera*, the cake invented by Gaston Lenôtre himself. And what a cake! Very thin layers of génoise soaked with a powerful coffee-flavored syrup, spread with equally thin layers of creamy coffee mousse, and finished with a neat chocolate glaze. There is none better.

And there's a gorgeous collection of dipped chocolates too: Creole, with rum-raisin ganache, Citrus with four different crystallized fruits, and ultrathin curved *tuiles au chocolat*, arcs of chocolate and finely chopped toasted almonds.

The Ecole Lenôtre located on the outskirts of Paris, is considered the home of the best pastry training classes anywhere. Classes for nonprofessionals can be arranged at their classrooms in Paris, through their website.

Lenôtre

48, ave Victor Hugo, 16th
Métro: Victor Hugo
01.45.02.21.21
www.lenotre.fr

THE BOULANGER

Although known primarily for his superlative breads, Eric Kayser produces some terrific chocolate pastries, including an unusual chocolate *financier*: tiny buttons of cake, rich with ground almonds and lots of dark chocolate, one of my favorite *goûtes* in Paris. Also order a dense square of *tarte au chocolat*, sliced from an enormous rectangle. The *pain au chocolat* here are excellent.

Maison Kayser
8-14, rue Monge, 5th
Métro: Maubert-Mutualité
01.44.07.01.42

SCULPTURE SO GOOD YOU CAN TASTE IT

This immensely appealing cocoa-colored shop is filled with all sorts of chocolate treats. I've savored too many of Monsieur Chaudun's well-toasted almonds—heaps coated with dark chocolate—and my very special friends get his chocolate truffles, tiny pristine cubes arranged in neat rows within each precious box.

Another favorite is *Columb*, which contains crunchy flecks of roasted cacao beans. Chaudun is a master of chocolate sculpting, and you never know what ordinary object he'll make into a custom creation: cell phones, musical instruments, sausages, and more.

Michael Chaudun
149, rue de l'Université, 7th
Métro: Invalides
01.47.53.74.40

MEET THE MASTER

Don't even think about coming to Paris without at least one visit to Pierre Hermé's fantastic dessert shop. Every centimeter of this shop is used, whether for neat rows of cloudlike chocolate tarts, towering cherry cakes, or the filled showcases of chocolates, all of which are made behind the boutique. It's all very chic and sophisticated—and perhaps the best pastry shop in Paris!

Pierre Hermé
72, rue Bonaparte, 6th
Métro: St. Sulpice
01.43.54.47.77

the great book of chocolate

A TASTE OF MODERNITY

Michel Richart, a Lyon-based chocolatier, is known for ultrasleek and very modern chocolates, often accented with unusual flavors to complement the season. Each tiny carré is a picture-perfect confection, silk-screened with abstract designs using cocoa butter, and packed in multitiered square boxes. Flavors such as lemon verbena, star anise, Macvin wine from the Jura, honey, and jasmine are featured, but I always leave with a few squares of his dark chocolates filled with salted caramel, runny and unctuous.

Richart
258, boulevard St. Germain, 7th
Métro: Solférino
01.45.55.66.00
www.richart.com

EAST MEETS WEST

In possibly the most fascinating pastry shop in Paris, pastry chef Sadaharu Aoki blends traditional Japanese flavors, such as green tea, with chocolate, creating desserts with that play flavors against one another. This ultramodern, slender shop features black sesame seed truffles, squares of chocolate dusted with matcha green tea, and defiantly vertical cylinders of individual pillowy soft dark chocolate cakes.

Sadaharu Aoki
35, rue de Vaugirard, 6th
Métro: St. Placide or Rennes
01.45 44 48 90

MADE IN FRANCE

Big jars of colorful candies guard the entryway inside Sevant, a sweet haven discretely located in the bourgeois 16th arrondissement. This impressive shop carries only candies and chocolates, most made in France. Choose from bins of chocolate-covered nuts, crispy cookielike meringues, and bonbons. A visit to Sevant is a must for any candy-lover.

Sevant
30, rue d'Auteuil, 16th
Métro: Michel Ange d'Auteuil
01.42.88.49.82

Recipes

The following is a collection of recipes I've developed that reflect my love of chocolate. Many are completely new, while others are revisited and updated classics. I also gathered terrific chocolate recipes from my favorite bakeries, chocolate shops, restaurants, and chocolatiers, adapting them for the home cook.

Here you'll find everything from tender scones with tasty tidbits of chocolate and quivering chocolate custards to superstar brownies, indulgent bittersweet truffles, and moist cakes that range from a suave 3-ingredient Chocolate number to a gooey all-American Mocha Pudding Cake. Plus, I've included a few savory recipes for those of us who can't ever get enough chocolate.

It goes without saying that the best things to eat are made from the best ingredients, and chocolate desserts are no exception. Treat yourself with the finest chocolate you can find. Browse everyday and upscale groceries, natural food stores, and ethnic markets, and peruse the Internet (see page 153) for unfamiliar, intriguing, rare, or exotic chocolates. Then follow along with me as I melt, dip, fold, and frost...

Allowing for Variation

Although the times, temperatures, and pan sizes given in the following recipes have been tested and standardized, your oven may vary from mine so use your judgment when testing for doneness. If you substitute a different-sized pan or baking dish, you'll need to adjust the cooking time accordingly. And always use an oven thermometer; I've seen considerable variations in oven accuracy during my baking career.

USEFUL TIPS FOR WORKING WITH CHOCOLATE

If you're new to working with chocolate, please read the tips on the next pages; they provide valuable information for successful baking.

Chopping Chocolate

If you have a large block of chocolate, the best method of chopping it into smaller pieces is to place the block on a sturdy cutting surface. Using a serrated knife (such as a bread knife), hold your fingers high away from the blade, and use a rocking and downward motion to chip small chunks from a corner (it's easier to cut corners than to cut through the length of a big chocolate bar). Continue to cut, shaving the chocolate into splinters. Once you've chipped away at the corner so it's no longer a corner anymore, rotate the block and work on another corner until you have as much chocolate as you need.

For really big, thick blocks of chocolate, I put the block into a sturdy plastic bag and whack it with a hammer until it's in manageable pieces. Since it's always more economical to buy premium quality chocolate in bulk, I recommend buying it this way and storing the chunks in a airtight plastic container in a cool, dark place.

Melting Chocolate

For fast, even melting, the chocolate pieces should be as small as possible. I like pieces to be no larger than rough, $1/2$-inch (1.3 cm) chunks.

Make sure you use a clean, dry bowl for melting pure chocolate. Just a drop of liquid can cause your chocolate to seize and become unworkable. If this happens, you won't be able to use it for dipping, but you can salvage it to make chocolate sauce by adding about half as much milk, water, coffee, or cream as the amount of chocolate you were melting. Overheating chocolate can also cause it to become grainy. To avoid this, keep an eye on your chocolate while it's melting, a reason I avoid using a microwave. You can't watch it while it heats, and chocolate deceptively holds its shape while warming in a microwave, giving no indication of how hot the interior is getting. If you overheat chocolate, you can sometimes strain out the hardened bits, but be sure to taste it, making sure there's no burnt taste left behind.

To melt chocolate on the stovetop, add pieces of chocolate to a heatproof bowl. Set the pan over a saucepan of barely simmering water and stir the chocolate gently until melted. Remove the bowl of chocolate from atop the saucepan carefully and wipe the bottom of the bowl dry with a kitchen towel, making sure no steam curls up around the sides and into the bowl, getting into the chocolate and causing it to seize.

Why Is My Chocolate Seizing?

One thing that can be vexing to a baker or confectioner is having chocolate seize. This is sometimes caused by overheating, when the melted chocolate gets too hot and little hard lumps form in the chocolate.

A more common cause of chocolate seizing is when a small amount of liquid is accidentally added to the chocolate. Chocolate has a lot of cocoa butter, and most cooks discover that oil and water don't mix. In her excellent book *Cookwise*, food scientist and cook Shirley Corriher likens the phenomena of chocolate seizing from a small amount of liquid to placing a damp spoon in a sugar bowl, which causes the sugar to become hard and granular; but by stirring in more water, you can make either mixture smooth.

Adding too little liquid (or even butter, which is about 20% water) will likely cause the chocolate to lose its smoothness and become a granular mass. If you want to add flavor to pure melted chocolate, don't use extracts. Use flavored oils such as peppermint, anise, or any edible oil. And some professionals add cocoa butter (available from Sweet Celebrations, page 90) to decrease the viscosity without altering the flavor.

The rule of thumb is that if you need to melt chocolate with a liquid, there should be at least 25% of the liquid to the chocolate. For example, if you melt 4 ounces of chocolate, you should have at least 2 tablespoons of liquid or butter.

You can melt chocolate either in a double boiler, as mentioned before, or in the microwave.

Using a microwave, chocolate should ideally be melted at medium power (which I've yet to figure out on my microwave—all those dials and buttons!). Open the door every 15 seconds and stir it because microwaved chocolate will not melt into a smooth mass without being stirred and so will not look melted until you stir it.

Tempering Chocolate

The most basic method of tempering chocolate, whether dark, milk, or white, is done in several steps. Although there are several reportedly "quick" methods for tempering chocolate, I've experimented and found just about all of them can result in improperly tempered chocolate. The method that I use is foolproof, provided you use an accurate thermometer. If you can't get a chocolate thermometer, an easy-to-read digital one will work. Chocolate thermometers are available at candy-making shops as well as at Sweet Celebrations (www.sweetc.com) and at Sur La Table stores (www.surla table.com).

A fun tempering project is the recipe for Rocky Road (page 144), as it is easy to enrobe an entire bowl of ingredients at once rather than dipping chocolates piece by piece and having to maintain the chocolate at the proper temperature for the duration of dipping. Although it may sound a bit long-winded, I'm overexplaining it just a bit to help you understand, but it's just three basic steps: melting, cooling, and rewarming. Here's my foolproof method for tempering chocolate:

1. Melt the chopped chocolate in a clean, dry bowl until it is fully melted and smooth. Remove the bowl of chocolate from the heat and drop a chunk of tempered chocolate (the chocolate you buy in bar form is tempered) into the bowl. The chunk should be roughly 25% of the amount you melted.

2. Allow the melted chocolate to cool down to the low 80°F range (upper 20°C range), stirring it every now and then to speed cooling.

3. Once cooled, the seed is removed (and saved to be remelted or chopped into pieces and incorporated into a dough) and the chocolate is carefully reheated to between 88°F and 91°F (31°C and 33°C), a range given by most manufacturers for dark chocolate, although some vary, so check the package for information, if available. Milk and white chocolate are in temper when between 86°F and 88°F (30°C and 31°C). This careful reheating should be done in 3- to 5-second intervals, by setting the bowl of chocolate over a saucepan of simmering water, then removing the bowl from the heat and checking the temperature. I call this "flashing." If you leave the bowl over the water until a thermometer reads the correct temperature, it will continue to rise too much after you remove it from the heat and you will need to begin the tempering process all over again. And be sure to use a dry towel to wipe moisture from the bottom of the bowl as you remove it from the heat. Do not be impatient at this point, since it will take just a few times of flashing the chocolate over the heat to bring the temperature up.

Now that your chocolate is tempered, you can dip, coat, and swirl it as needed, but work quickly because it will hold the proper temperature for only a couple of minutes. If you maintain the temperature between 88°F and 91°F (31°C and 33°C), you can work away at a more leisurely pace. Some home cooks use a heating pad to maintain the correct temperature. If it cools to below 88°F (31°C), very gently rewarm the chocolate, and continue to use it. Professional chocolate shops usually have tempering kettles, which provide a steady supply of tempered chocolate to fill chocolate molds and create decorations. Large factories have immense tempering kettles, which temper the chocolate in bulk before it is deposited into molds. Tempering machines designed for home cooks that temper and sustain a temper for about $1^{1}/_{2}$ pounds (about .7 kg) of chocolate at a time are available from kitchenware purveyors.

Using the Right Chocolate

Do not interchange natural cocoa powder for Dutch-process cocoa powder. Use what the recipe specifies. One is acidic and the other is alkali. If you don't have Dutch-process cocoa, chocolate guru Nick Malgieri advises adding a pinch of baking soda to the cocoa powder. Unsweetened cocoa powder is not the same thing as ground chocolate (see page 32). They cannot be used interchangeably in recipes.

Bitter chocolate is unsweetened chocolate. Bittersweet chocolate is sweetened, with added cocoa butter. Bitter and bittersweet chocolate behave very differently in recipes and are not interchangeable.

Using Nuts

When toasted nuts are called for, spread raw nuts on a baking sheet and toast in a preheated 350°F (175°C) oven for about 10 minutes, stirring once or twice to make sure they are browning evenly. To test doneness, snap open a nut: it should break cleanly and the inside should be lightly browned throughout. Nuts contain a lot of natural oil and can turn rancid easily. Taste a few to make sure the ones you are using are fresh tasting.

Cherry, Chocolate, and Buttermilk Scones

18 MEDIUM-SIZED SCONES

These scones are full of flavor and have a fine crumbly texture due to tender cake flour and restrained kneading. Carolyn Weil, who owned a very popular bakery in Berkeley, California, for many years, passed on this recipe for the scones that used to fly out of her ovens, nourishing morning snackers and passing commuters hungry for a good dose of chocolate first thing in the morning. For a sweet-crunchy topping, I liberally dust the scones with lots of sugar and a few wisps of cinnamon before baking.

- 1 cup [140 grams] all-purpose flour
- 1 cup [140 grams] cake flour
- $1/4$ cup [50 grams] sugar
- 2 teaspoons baking powder
- $1/2$ teaspoon baking soda
- $1/4$ teaspoon salt
- 1 teaspoon orange zest
- 8 tablespoons (1 stick) [115 grams] unsalted butter, cold
- $3/4$ cup [90 grams] dried cherries, sweet or sour
- $1/2$ cup [60 grams] miniature chocolate chips
- $2/3$ cup [170 ml] buttermilk

Cinnamon Sugar for Topping
- 3 tablespoons sugar
- $1/4$ teaspoon cinnamon

Preheat the oven to 375°F (190°C). Line a baking sheet with parchment paper. Lightly flour a work surface.

•

In a large bowl, mix the flours, sugar, baking powder, baking soda, salt, and orange zest with a wire whisk.

•

Cut the butter into $1/2$-inch (1.3-cm) cubes and add to the flour mixture. Using the paddle of a stand mixer or your fingers or a pastry cutter, cut the butter into the flour mixture until it is a fine texture and looks a little like cornmeal with evenly dispersed chunks of butter.

•

Stir in the cherries, chocolate chips, and buttermilk, stirring just until the moment the dough becomes wet and sticky.

•

(continued)

Turn the dough out onto the floured work surface and pat it into a 1-inch (2.5-cm) thick circle. Cut the circle into 8 wedges. Mix the cinnamon and sugar together on a small plate. Press the top of each wedge heavily into the sugar mixture and place the scones evenly spaced on the baking sheet with the sugared side on top.

•

Bake until firm to the touch on top and lightly golden brown, 15 to 20 minutes. Serve warm.

•

Variation: Substitute an equal amount of dried currants, cranberries, diced dried California apricots, or any other dried fruit for the dried cherries.

•

The dry ingredient mixture in the second step will hold in the refrigerator for days when sealed in a resealable plastic bag. This makes it easy to finish off the scones in the early morning, simple enough to do before you've had your morning coffee and when your eyes are still only half open.

the great book of chocolate

Chocolate Shortbread Hearts

20 COOKIES

Baker and food writer Fran Gage is a neighbor of mine in San Francisco. Although I have never had to stop by to borrow a cup of sugar (or a pound of chocolate), it's comforting to know that she's right there in case the need arises. And I certainly wouldn't mind if she came by sometime, even unannounced, if she brought a platter of her snappy and sexy Chocolate Shortbread Hearts.

1 3/4 cups [245 grams] all-purpose flour

1/2 cup [50 grams] unsweetened Dutch-process cocoa powder

1/4 teaspoon salt

1/2 pound (2 sticks) [230 grams] unsalted butter, at room temperature

1 1/4 cups [125 grams] powdered sugar

Sift together the flour, cocoa, and salt.

•

Beat together the butter and powdered sugar just until mixed. Do not overbeat. Add the flour mixture and stir just until combined.

•

Flatten the dough into a 1-inch (2.5-cm) thick rectangle and cover it tightly with plastic wrap. Refrigerate for at least 1 hour.

•

Line a baking sheet with parchment paper. Adjust the rack to the center of the oven and preheat to 325°F (160°C).

•

On a very lightly floured surface, roll the dough until 1/4 inch (6 mm) thick. Avoid using much flour, which will cloud the cookies' chocolaty appearance and give them a tough texture. (Use a pastry brush to whisk away any excess.)

•

Use a 3-inch (7.5-cm) heart-shaped cookie cutter to cut individual cookies from the dough. Arrange the cookies on the prepared baking sheet. (Dough scraps can be rerolled once and cut into additional hearts.)

•

Bake for 12 to 15 minutes, until the cookies are set but not hard.

•

Cool on a rack.

•

Although best when eaten the same day, these cookies can be stored overnight at room temperature in an airtight container.

Bouchons

12 INDIVIDUAL CAKES

I first visited Portland's Pearl Bakery by accident. I was taking a stroll through the historic Pearl District when I passed a bustling bakery that looked like a find. Later I learned that the Pearl Bakery was already quite well-known to just about everyone else but me. During my visit, I ordered a *Bouchon* along with a heaped platter of their tasty treats, which I promptly devoured. The chocolate *Bouchon*, with its crumbly, melt-in-your-mouth texture, was the best of all, especially when accompanied with a cup of very strong, very dark coffee, as they drink in Portland. Thanks to baker Lee Posey for sharing this terrific recipe.

3 1/2 ounces [100 grams] bittersweet or semisweet chocolate, chopped

3 1/2 ounces [100 grams] unsweetened chocolate, chopped

1/2 pound (2 sticks) [230 grams] unsalted butter, at room temperature

1 1/4 cup [250 grams] sugar

4 large eggs, at room temperature

1 3/4 cup [245 grams] cake flour

1 1/2 tablespoons unsweetened cocoa powder, natural or Dutch-process

Pinch of salt

3/4 cup [90 grams] miniature chocolate chips

Adjust the rack to the center of the oven and preheat to 375°F (190°C). Butter a 12-cup muffin pan.

•

In a heatproof bowl set over a pan of simmering water, melt the bittersweet and unsweetened chocolate together.

•

In the bowl of an electric mixer, beat the butter and sugar until very light and fluffy. Add the eggs one at a time, beating well after each addition. Mix in the melted chocolate.

•

Sift together the flour, cocoa powder, and salt.

•

Stir the dry ingredients into the chocolate mixture in 3 additions, then stir in the chocolate chips.

•

Fill each muffin cup with batter and bake for 18 minutes, or until they still feel quite soft in their centers when lightly pressed with a fingertip. Do not overbake.

•

Remove from the oven, cool for 10 minutes, then remove the cakes from the muffin tin.

•

These are best eaten the day they are made, but they're still good served the following day. Store at room temperature in an airtight container.

Wittamer Hot Chocolate

ABOUT 1 QUART (1 LITER)

This recipe is a soothing winter warm-up from Wittamer (page 57), in Brussels, courtesy of Michael Lewis-Anderson. In their smart tea salon, they serve this satisfying hot chocolate during the holiday season so their customers can take a relaxing break from shopping in the chic shops around the place du Grand Sablon. And just in case you're one of those people like me who can't ever get enough Belgian chocolate, a few creamy chocolates from the shop downstairs are served alongside. If you're unaccustomed to Belgian richness, use milk instead of the half-and-half. At Wittamer, this hot chocolate is spooned into mugs and served with a swirl of whipped cream and lacy chocolate curls.

> 1 quart [1 liter] half-and-half (or whole milk)
> 8 ounces [225 grams] bittersweet or semisweet chocolate, chopped
> 4 ounces [115 grams] milk chocolate, chopped
> 1/2 teaspoon ground cinnamon

In a saucepan, heat 1 cup (250 ml) of the half-and-half with the dark and milk chocolates. Stir until melted. Add the remaining half-and-half and the cinnamon and heat.

•

Stir briskly with a whisk or use an immersion blender to make the hot chocolate completely smooth.

Deep Dark Chocolate Truffles

25 TO 30 TRUFFLES

These truffles were inspired by the amazingly intense, decadent chocolates that abound in Belgium. This is a fun, hands-on project that will make you feel like a skilled chocolatier even if you are normally a disaster in the kitchen. Be sure to clean and thoroughly dry your hands before rolling and dipping the truffles. These are great to serve after dinner with a nice Armagnac or espresso. During holidays, I package truffles in gold-flecked gift bags (available at Sweet Celebrations, page 90) to placate to chocolate-loving friends.

3/4 cup [185 ml] heavy cream

8 to 10 ounces [225 to 285 grams] bittersweet or semisweet chocolate, chopped

1 to 3 teaspoons cognac, to taste (or another favorite liquor)

Coating

4 ounces [115 grams] bittersweet or semisweet chocolate, chopped

1/2 cup [50 grams] unsweetened cocoa powder

In a small saucepan, bring the cream just to a boil. Remove from the heat and stir in the chocolate, stirring until melted. Add the liquor and pour into a bowl. Let stand for at least 2 hours or until firm. (Or chill, covered, until firm, but allow to warm slightly before scooping.)

•

Using a melon baller (or a soup spoon), dip the melon-baller in a bowl of very warm water, tap off excess water, and scoop the truffle mixture into 3/4-inch (2-cm) balls and set them on a plate. Once you've scooped all the mixture, roll each one with your hands until round.

•

Chill the truffles thoroughly.

•

Melt the 4 ounces (115 grams) of bittersweet chocolate in a heatproof bowl set over a pan of simmering water. Spread the cocoa powder in a pie plate.

•

Spread some of the melted chocolate into your right hand. (Reverse this if you're left-handed.) Pick up a truffle with your clean left hand and place it into your chocolate-covered right hand. Smear chocolate all over the truffle with your right hand and then drop it into the cocoa powder. Repeat until the truffles fill the pie plate, keeping your left hand clean to keep lifting the truffles. Shake the pie plate to cover the truffles with cocoa powder, then place them in a strainer to shake off the excess cocoa. Repeat to enrobe the remaining truffles.

•

Once dipped, the truffles can be served immediately or can be refrigerated for up to 10 days. Remove from the refrigerator at least 1 hour before serving.

Chocolate Fitness Cake

6 SERVINGS

I can't keep up with all the fitness fads and diets that come and go, but this powerful chocolate cake always satisfies—no matter which health regimen you may be following. It's a compact cake that sports a lean line-up of only three ingredients, yet it still bulges with Herculean chocolate flavor.

- 3/4 cup [75 grams] unsweetened cocoa powder, natural or Dutch-process
- 1/2 cup plus 3 tablespoons [100 grams plus 35 grams] granulated sugar
- 7 large egg whites, at room temperature

Preheat the oven to 325°F (160°C).

•

Butter a 2-quart (2-liter) soufflé mold or similar-sized oven-proof baking dish or bowl. Sift or whisk together the cocoa powder and the 1/2 cup (100 grams) of sugar to remove any lumps.

•

Whip the egg whites until they form soft, droopy peaks. Whip in the remaining 3 tablespoons (35 grams) of sugar. Carefully fold in the cocoa mixture in 3 batches, just until incorporated, stopping just before the mixture becomes smooth. Do not overfold.

•

Transfer the mixture into the soufflé mold or baking dish. Set the mold in a larger pan. Add warm water to the larger pan, so that the water reaches 1 to 2 inches (2.5 to 5 cm) up the outside of the mold, creating a water bath.

•

Bake for 35 to 40 minutes, until the cake is barely set in the center.

•

Remove the cake from the water bath. Wait 5 minutes, then invert it onto a serving plate and serve.

•

Chocolate Fitness Cake is lovely served warm, although it can be served at room temperature and will keep 2 days if wrapped in plastic. I like it topped with orange segments drizzled with honey, or (if you're less virtuous) with Fresh Mint and White Chocolate Crème Anglaise (page 129).

Chocolate Soufflé Cake

ONE 9-INCH (23-CM) CAKE, 8 TO 12 SERVINGS

This cake will rise gloriously as it bakes, then exhale and settle nicely into a moist, fudgy dessert. Nothing could be easier to make, and I make it often because I always have the few ingredients at hand. It's great with vanilla-scented whipped cream, or a scoop of vanilla or espresso ice cream enlivened with a drizzle of nice cognac or dark rum.

Filling

> 15 ounces [425 grams] bittersweet or semisweet chocolate, chopped
>
> 15 tablespoons (1$7/8$ sticks) [210 grams] unsalted butter, cut into small pieces
>
> 5 large eggs, at room temperature
>
> $1/2$ cup [100 grams] sugar

Adjust the oven rack to the center of the oven and preheat to 375°F (190°C). Butter a 9-inch (23-cm) springform cake pan.

•

In a medium-sized heatproof bowl set over a pan of simmering water, melt the chocolate and the butter until smooth, stirring frequently.

•

Remove from the heat.

•

Beat the eggs and sugar with an electric mixer until they are thick and foam, and hold their shape when the beater is lifted.

•

Fold the eggs into the chocolate mixture, folding until no streaks of egg white remain. Transfer the filling into the prepared cake pan.

•

Bake for 30 minutes.

•

Let the cake cool in the pan until completely cool, then cut and serve.

•

This cake is best served the same day.

Orange and Rum Chocolate Mousse Cake

ONE 8-INCH (21-CM) CAKE, 12 SERVINGS

This recipe is from Nick Malgieri, cookbook author and expert on all things chocolate. His book, *Chocolate: From Simple Cookies to Extravagant Showstoppers* oozes chocolate with its whimsical chocolate cobblestone house and elegant candies and cookies, as well as dazzling dark chocolate cakes. This recipe is one of his favorite chocolate fixes. It's simple to make, and quite rich—so much so that when Nick gave me the recipe he was sure to say that this makes 12 "very rich servings." Because this cake is so rich, it's best served with a simple mound of very lightly sweetened whipped cream.

1 cup [250 ml] water

^{1}/2 cup [100 grams] sugar

8 tablespoons (1 stick) [115 grams] unsalted butter, cut into pieces

10 ounces [285 grams] 70% cacao bittersweet chocolate, chopped

6 large eggs

Grated zest of 1 orange

1 to 2 tablespoons dark rum

Preheat the oven to 325°F (160°C). Butter an 8 x 2-inch (20 x 5-cm) round cake pan. Line the bottom with a disk of parchment paper cut to fit.

•

Heat the water and sugar in a medium saucepan. Once the sugar is dissolved and the syrup begins to simmer, remove from the heat and stir in the butter, then the chocolate. Mix until the chocolate has completely melted.

•

In a large mixing bowl, whisk the eggs together with the orange zest and rum. Gradually whisk in the chocolate mixture.

•

Transfer the batter to the prepared cake pan. Set the cake pan in a large pan (such as a roasting pan). Add warm water to the larger pan so that the water reaches about 1 inch (2.5 cm) up the outside of the cake pan, creating a water bath.

•

Bake for 45 minutes, or until the batter is slightly risen and soft, but feels just firm, and no longer liquid, in the center.

•

Remove the cake from the water bath and cool on a wire rack. Once cool, invert the cake onto a serving plate, remove the pan, and peel off the parchment paper.

•

This cake can be made and chilled up to 3 days before serving. Allow it to return to room temperature before serving.

Black-Bottom Cupcakes

12 CUPCAKES

These yummy classics deserve a revival. Who doesn't like individual, moist, and deep red devil's food cakes with a creamy cheesecake filling? Children like them in lunch boxes. And adults (like me) enjoy them for breakfast.

Filling

- 8 ounces [225 grams] cream cheese, regular or reduced fat, at room temperature
- 1/3 cup [65 grams] granulated sugar
- 1 large egg, at room temperature
- 2 ounces [60 grams] bittersweet or semisweet chocolate, coarsely chopped

Cupcakes

- 1 1/2 cups [210 grams] all-purpose flour
- 1 cup [240 grams] firmly packed light brown sugar
- 5 tablespoons [30 grams] natural unsweetened cocoa powder (not Dutch-process)
- 1 teaspoon baking soda
- 1/4 teaspoon salt
- 1 cup [250 ml] water
- 1/3 cup [85 ml] unflavored vegetable oil
- 1 tablespoon white or cider vinegar
- 1 teaspoon vanilla extract

(continued)

Adjust the rack to the center of the oven and preheat to 350°F (175°C). Butter a 12-cup muffin tin, or line the tin with paper muffin cups.

•

To make the filling, beat together the cream cheese, granulated sugar, and egg until smooth. Stir in the chopped chocolate pieces. Set aside.

•

To make the cupcake batter, in a medium bowl sift together the flour, brown sugar, cocoa powder, baking soda, and salt. In a separate bowl, mix together the water, oil, vinegar, and vanilla.

•

Make a well in the center of the dry ingredients and stir in the wet ingredients, stirring until just smooth. Stir any longer and you will overmix the batter and end up with less-than-tender cupcakes.

•

Divide the batter among the muffin cups. Spoon a few table-spoons of the filling into the center of each cupcake, dividing the filling evenly. This will fill the cups almost completely, which is fine.

•

Bake for 25 minutes, or until the tops are slightly golden brown and the cupcakes feel springy when gently pressed.

•

These moist treats will keep well unrefrigerated for 2 to 3 days if stored in an airtight container.

the great book of chocolate

Blue Chip Chocolate Chip Cookies

ABOUT 20 COOKIES

Here's a supersecret recipe from a famous now-shuttered San Francisco cookie shop, Blue Chip Cookies, which was appropriately located in Ghirardelli Square, the site of the city's oldest chocolate factory. Many fondly remember the shop's terrific (and huge) chocolate chip cookies. There are lots of stories circulating about famous chocolate chip cookie recipes from department stores and cookie shops, all of them the stuff of urban myths. But this recipe is the real thing. Its authenticity was assured by local baker John Carroll, who stowed away a copy of the recipe, written on the bakery's original letterhead. There is nothing ordinary about these cookies. One bite and you'll be convinced that they're the stuff legends *are* made of.

- 1/2 cup [100 grams] granulated sugar
- 1/2 cup [120 grams] firmly packed light brown sugar
- 8 tablespoons (1 stick) [115 grams] unsalted butter, cold, cut into 1/2-inch [1-cm] pieces
- 1 large egg
- 1 teaspoon vanilla extract
- 1/2 teaspoon baking soda
- 1 1/4 cups [175 grams] all-purpose flour
- 1/4 teaspoon salt
- 1 1/2 cups [200 grams] semisweet chocolate chips
- 1 cup [130 grams] walnuts or pecans, toasted (see page 91) and chopped

Adjust the oven rack to the top third of the oven and preheat to 300°F (150°C). Line 3 baking sheets with parchment paper.

•

Beat the sugars and butter together until smooth. Mix in the egg, vanilla, and baking soda.

•

Stir together the flour and salt, then mix them into the batter. Mix in the chocolate chips and nuts.

•

Scoop the cookie dough into 2-tablespoon (5-cm) balls and place 8 balls, spaced 4 inches (10 cm) apart, on each of the baking sheets.

•

Bake for 18 minutes, or until pale golden brown. Remove from the oven and cool on a wire rack.

•

Store at room temperature in an airtight container for up to 3 days.

Double Chocolate Espresso and Cashew Cookies

ABOUT 24 COOKIES

You can use either regular or Dutched cocoa powder in these divine domes o' heaven. If you don't want to eat or serve them all at once, go ahead and scoop the dough into round portions on a plate lined with plastic wrap. Freeze, then transfer the frozen dough balls to a resealable plastic bag. When you need to satisfy your chocolate cravings in short order, separate the balls on a baking sheet, thaw a few minutes, and bake. This recipe comes from Letty Flatt, who is the head baker at the Deer Valley resort in the mountains of Utah, which, along with these excellent cookies, I believe is quite close to heaven.

1/2 pound (2 sticks) [230 grams] unsalted butter, softened

1 cup [200 grams] granulated sugar

3/4 cup [180 grams] firmly packed light brown sugar

2 large eggs

1 teaspoon pure vanilla extract

2 teaspoons instant espresso powder

2 cups [280 grams] all-purpose flour

2/3 cup [65 grams] natural unsweetened cocoa powder (not Dutch-process)

1 teaspoon baking soda

1 teaspoon salt

3/4 cup [100 grams] cashews, toasted (see page 91) and chopped

3/4 cup [100 grams] semisweet chocolate chips

Preheat the oven to 325°F (160°C). Line 3 baking sheets with parchment paper or oil them lightly with vegetable oil.

•

In a large bowl, using an electric mixer, cream the butter and sugars until light and fluffy. Add the eggs, vanilla , and espresso powder. Mix well, stopping once to scrape the sides and bottom of the bowl.

•

Sift together the flour, cocoa powder, baking soda, and salt. Mix into the creamed butter mixture, scraping again. Stir in the cashews and chocolate chips.

•

Scoop the cookie dough into large (1/4-cup [4-cm]) balls, arranging them at least 2 inches (5 cm) apart, 8 on each baking sheet. Bake until the cookies are just flat, 20 to 25 minutes, turning and rotating the baking sheets as necessary for even baking.

•

Let cool about 10 minutes before transferring from the baking sheet to the cooling rack.

•

Once cool, store at room temperature in an airtight container for up to 3 days.

Congo Bars

24 BARS

Cookbook author Flo Braker, who gave me this recipe, told me this was her most requested recipe ever. She recommends keeping them for a few days before eating them. This was something I was unable to verify, as they lasted less than one afternoon in my house each time I tried to test her advice.

11 tablespoons (about 1^1/$_3$ sticks) [150 grams] unsalted butter, melted and cooled

1 pound [450 grams] light brown sugar

3 large eggs

2^3/$_4$ cups [385 grams] all-purpose flour

2^1/$_2$ teaspoons baking powder

^{1}/$_2$ teaspoon salt

2 cups [280 grams] semisweet chocolate chips

1 cup [130 grams] walnuts or pecans, toasted (see page 91) and chopped

Adjust the rack to the lower third of the oven and preheat to 325°F (160°C).

•

Butter a 10 x 15 x 1-inch (25 x 38 x 2.5-cm) baking pan.

•

In a large bowl, mix the butter, brown sugar, and eggs, making sure to break up any lumps of brown sugar.

•

In a separate bowl, sift together the flour, baking powder, and salt. Mix the dry ingredients into the egg mixture, then stir in the chocolate chips and nuts.

•

Spread the batter into the pan as evenly as possible. (It will be sticky; I suggest using your fingers to pat it out.)

•

Bake for 20 minutes, or until deep golden brown. Remove from the oven. Let cool a few minutes, and then cut into 24 bars while still warm.

•

Although you'll find it hard to resist eating all of them right away, Flo insists that the bars actually improve after a few days when stored at room temperature in an airtight container.

the great book of chocolate

Dave and Kate's Remarkable Brownies

16 BROWNIES

This recipe for Katharine Hepburn's brownies cropped up in my file when I was selecting recipes for this book. I am told that at the time she was making them, they were considered as legendary as the woman herself. Her family lived just around the bend from mine in Connecticut. I was happy to know that we also had a love of good brownies in common.

Ms. Hepburn's recipe was fine as it was, but tastes have changed over the years so I tweaked it here and there, adding more chocolate as well as a handful of chocolate chips. But like Kate herself, the original spirit is indomitable and I think she'd agree that Dave and Kate's brownies are the product of a perfect partnership.

> 8 tablespoons (1 stick) [115 grams] unsalted butter
>
> 4 ounces [115 grams] unsweetened chocolate, chopped
>
> 1 cup [200 grams] sugar
>
> 2 large eggs
>
> 1/2 teaspoon vanilla extract
>
> 6 tablespoons [50 grams] all-purpose flour
>
> 1/4 teaspoon salt
>
> 3/4 cup [100 grams] walnuts or pecans, toasted (see page 91) and chopped
>
> 1/2 cup [70 grams] semisweet chocolate chips

Butter an 8-inch (20-cm) square cake pan and lightly dust it with flour, tapping out any excess. Adjust the oven rack to the center of the oven and preheat to 325°F (160°C).

•

In a medium saucepan, melt the butter. Add the chopped chocolate and stir over low heat until melted. Remove from the heat and mix in the sugar, then the eggs and vanilla.

•

Stir in the flour and salt, then the nuts and chocolate chips. Scrape the brownie mixture into the prepared pan and bake for 30 minutes. Remove from the oven and cool on a wire rack.

•

The original recipe said to cut the cooled brownies into neat squares and eat them right out of the pan. Or store them at room temperature in an airtight container for up to 3 days.

Downtown Bakery Brownies

16 BROWNIES

I was lucky to work with Kathleen Stewart back when she waited tables at Chez Panisse, before she left to open the quintessential country bakery in Healdsburg, California, the Downtown Bakery and Creamery, where she makes these amazing brownies. I know that she will kill me for revealing her lesser known past here in print, but in addition to being a great baker, Kathleen was one of Dean Martin's ultraglamorous and voluptuous "Gold-diggers." Maybe it would have been more fitting for me to have asked her for her cheesecake brownie recipe.

Brownies

- 8 tablespoons (1 stick) [115 grams] unsalted butter, cut into small pieces
- 4 ounces [115 grams] unsweetened chocolate, chopped
- 1 cup [200 grams] sugar
- 2 large eggs
- 1 teaspoon vanilla extract
- 3/4 cup [105 grams] all-purpose flour
- 1/2 cup [65 grams] walnuts or pecans, toasted (see page 91) and chopped

Ganache Icing

- 1/4 cup [60 ml] heavy cream
- 2 ounces [60 grams] bittersweet or semisweet chocolate, chopped

Adjust the oven rack to the center of the oven and preheat to 325°F (160°C). Butter an 8-inch (20-cm) square cake pan.

•

In a medium saucepan over low heat, melt the butter and unsweetened chocolate, stirring often. Remove from the heat and stir in the sugar, then the eggs and the vanilla.

•

Mix in the flour and nuts. Scrape the batter into the prepared pan, smooth the top, and bake for 25 minutes.

•

Cool the brownies completely in the pan on a wire rack.

•

To make the ganache, warm the heavy cream and chocolate, stirring until smooth. Let cool briefly, until spreadable. Ice the brownies with the ganache either while still in the pan, or after they're removed from the pan and cut into squares.

Cocoa-Marzipan Pound Cake

TWO 8^1/$_2$-INCH (22-CM) LOAF CAKES,
ABOUT 16 SERVINGS

Is there anyone who appreciates almond paste more than I do? Having that can (or tube) of almond paste in the pantry is like having that "little black dress" in your closet. Here I use almond paste to flavor a rich chocolate pound cake, adding moisture and finesse.

^{3}/$_4$ cup (7 ounces) [200 grams] almond paste

1 cup [200 grams] sugar

^{1}/$_2$ teaspoon almond extract

1^1/$_2$ cups [210 grams] all-purpose flour

^{1}/$_2$ cup [50 grams] unsweetened Dutch-process
   cocoa powder

1 teaspoon baking powder

^{1}/$_2$ teaspoon salt

^{1}/$_2$ pound (2 sticks) [230 grams] unsalted butter,
   at room temperature

4 large eggs, at room temperature

^{1}/$_2$ cup [125 ml] milk

^{2}/$_3$ cup [100 grams] sliced almonds (optional)

Butter two 8^1/$_2$-inch (22-cm) loaf pans and dust with flour, tapping out any excess. Preheat the oven to 325°F (160°C).

•

In the bowl of a stand mixer, beat the almond paste, sugar, and almond extract until the almond paste is broken up into very fine pieces.

•

In a separate bowl, sift together the flour, cocoa, baking powder, and salt.

•

Add the butter to the almond paste mixture and beat until light and fluffy. Add the eggs one at a time, beating well after each addition.

•

Stir in half of the dry ingredients, then the milk. Then mix in the remaining dry ingredients.

•

Divide the batter between the loaf pans and smooth the tops of the cakes.

•

Evenly sprinkle the tops with sliced almonds. Bake the cakes for 45 minutes, or until a toothpick inserted into the center comes out clean.

•

Cool completely on a wire rack.

•

Variation: For a truly moist experience, omit the sliced almonds on top of the cakes. Make a syrup by bringing to a boil ^{2}/$_3$ cup (170 ml) amaretto with 3 tablespoons of honey. When you remove the unadorned cakes from the oven, pour the warm amaretto syrup over the cakes, slipping a knife around the edges of the cakes to allow the juice to soak in along the sides. Cool the soaked cakes in the loaf pans.

•

Once you remove the cakes from the loaf pans, wrap them in plastic wrap overnight to allow the flavors to meld. These cakes will keep for up to 3 days at room temperature, or if double-wrapped, can be frozen for up to 1 month.

Chocolate, Cherry, and Vanilla Cake with Truffle Frosting

ONE 9-INCH (23-CM) CAKE, 12 SERVINGS

An important ingredient in chocolate is, surprisingly, vanilla, which is added to most chocolates manufactured around the world. Although chocolate and vanilla are constantly battling for popularity, this grand, luscious cake from Patricia Rain of The Vanilla Company provides a happy truce. Patricia is the unparalleled queen of vanilla, and she only uses the best-quality Mexican pure vanilla extract in the cake and you should, too. Floral Tahitian vanilla in the chocolate truffle frosting and filling enhances the fruitiness of the cherry filling. But as with chocolate, the region is less important than the goodness and purity of the vanilla.

Cake

- 2 cups [280 grams] all-purpose flour
- 1/2 cup [50 grams] unsweetened cocoa powder, preferably not Dutch-process
- 1 1/2 teaspoons baking soda
- 1/2 teaspoon salt
- 1 1/2 cups [375 ml] sour cream
- 1 1/2 cups [300 grams] sugar
- 4 large eggs, at room temperature
- 2 tablespoons (1/4 stick) [30 g] unsalted butter, melted
- 4 teaspoons pure Mexican vanilla extract

Truffle Frosting

- 1 cup [200 grams] sugar
- 1 cup [250 ml] heavy cream
- 4 ounces [115 grams] unsweetened chocolate, chopped
- 8 tablespoons (1 stick) [115 grams] unsalted butter, cut into small pieces
- 1 tablespoon pure Tahitian vanilla extract

Filling

- 2/3 cup [230 grams] cherry preserves (or raspberry)
- 2 tablespoons kirsch, framboise, or Chambord
- 2 teaspoons pure Tahitian vanilla extract

Preheat the oven to 350°F (175°C). Butter two 9-inch (23-cm) round cake pans.

•

In a large mixing bowl, sift together the flour, cocoa, baking soda, and salt.

•

In a separate, medium-sized mixing bowl, whisk together the sour cream, sugar, eggs, melted butter, and Mexican vanilla.

•

Stir the wet ingredients into the flour mixture, stirring just until combined.

•

Scrape half of the batter into each of the prepared pans and bake until the top springs back when gently pressed with a fingertip, 20 to 25 minutes.

•

Remove the pans from the oven and cool completely. While the cake is cooling, make the truffle frosting by heating the sugar and cream in a medium saucepan until it begins to boil. Reduce the heat and simmer for 8 minutes.

•

Remove from heat and stir in the chocolate, butter, and Tahitian vanilla until smooth. Chill the frosting until it is firm enough to spread, 2 to 3 hours.

•

To finish the cake, stir together the cherry preserves, liquor, and vanilla extract. Place one layer of cake on a serving plate. Spread the preserves over the cake layer, leaving a 1/2-inch (1.3 cm) border (allowing the preserves room to spread without overflowing onto the sides when you top with the second layer). Top with the second layer of cake. Spread the frosting over the top and sides of the cake.

•

This recipe makes a generous amount of frosting. If you'd like to get fancy, as Patricia sometimes does, you can pipe rosettes of frosting evenly spaced around the top of the cake and adorn each rosette with a fresh cherry or raspberry.

Chocolate Sauerkraut Cake with Chocolate Glaze

ONE BUNDT CAKE, ABOUT 12 SERVINGS

I've never met Maida Heatter but everyone I know tells me she is absolutely the most lovely woman they've ever met. Ask anyone who has ever baked from one of Maida's books, which are full of personal stories and glowing descriptions, and they'll say that she makes you feel as though you've just had a personal baking lesson from the grande dame of American cake making herself. She generously seasons her recipes with superlatives. Cakes are glorious, fabulous, towering, stunning, mile high, sinful, and over-the-top. I've adapted the recipe from one of her recipes and once you bake it, you'll be using superlatives, too.

Cake

- $2/3$ cup [170 ml] sauerkraut
- $1/2$ cup [50 grams] unsweetened Dutch-process cocoa powder
- 2 cups [280 grams] all-purpose flour
- 1 teaspoon baking powder
- 1 teaspoon baking soda
- $1/4$ teaspoon salt
- 10 tablespoons ($1^1/4$ sticks) [140 grams] unsalted butter, at room temperature
- $1^1/2$ cups [300 grams] sugar
- 3 large eggs, at room temperature
- 1 teaspoon vanilla extract
- 1 cup [250 ml] low-fat milk, cold

(continued)

Glaze

    4 ounces [115 grams] bittersweet or semisweet
       chocolate, chopped

    4 tablespoons ($1/2$ stick) [60 grams] unsalted
       butter, cut into pieces

    1 teaspoon light corn syrup

Put the sauerkraut in a bowl of cold water. Squeeze it a few
times, then drain off the water and gently squeeze the sauerkraut to remove most of the water. Chop it very fine with a
chef's knife or in a food processor.

•

Preheat the oven to 325°F (160°C). Butter a 12-cup (3-liter)
Bundt or tube cake pan.

•

Sift together the cocoa, flour, baking powder, baking soda,
and salt.

•

In the bowl of an electric mixer, or by hand, beat the butter
and sugar until light and creamy. In a separate bowl, beat the
eggs and vanilla. While beating the butter, slowly dribble in
the eggs.

•

Stir in one-third of the dry ingredients, then half of the milk.
Then stir in another third of the dry ingredients, then the
remaining milk. Finally, mix in the remaining dry ingredients,
and the chopped sauerkraut.

•

Transfer the batter to the prepared Bundt pan and bake for
45 minutes, or until a toothpick inserted into the center comes
out clean. Cool completely then invert onto a serving plate.

•

To make the glaze, heat the chocolate, butter, and corn syrup
together until melted and smooth. Let stand until room temperature, then spoon the glaze over the cooled cake, allowing it to run down the sides.

•

Mocha Pudding Cake

ONE 8-INCH (20-CM) CAKE, 6 TO 8 SERVINGS

**Several attempts to come up with a great pudding cake
made me realize that to get just the right texture, you
need to bake it less than you think you do. When it's
done, it will still appear quite jiggly in the center. You'll
swoon as you dive in. It's fun to make and not like any
other dessert I know—a marriage of pure chocolate and
coffee bliss. Serve warm, perhaps with a scoop of vanilla
ice cream or a dollop of sweetened whipped cream
flavored with a liqueur such as Kahlúa.**

> 1 cup [140 grams] all-purpose flour
>
> 1^1/2 cups [300 grams] sugar
>
> 6 tablespoons plus ^{1}/4 cup [40 grams plus 25 grams]
>   unsweetened cocoa powder, natural or Dutch-
>   process
>
> 1 teaspoon baking powder
>
> ^{1}/2 teaspoon salt
>
> 2 large eggs, at room temperature
>
> 2 tablespoons (^{1}/4 stick) [30 grams] butter, melted
>
> ^{1}/2 cup [125 ml] milk
>
> 1 teaspoon vanilla extract
>
> 1 cup [250 ml] hot, very strong, great-quality
>   brewed coffee

Adjust the rack to the center of the oven and preheat to
350°F (175°C). Butter an 8-inch (20-cm) square cake pan or a
2-quart (2-liter) shallow baking dish.

•

Sift together the flour, 1 cup (200 grams) of the sugar, the
6 tablespoons (40 grams) cocoa, baking powder, and salt.

•

In a medium bowl, mix together the eggs, melted butter, milk,
and vanilla.

•

Stir the liquid ingredients into the dry ingredients until just
combined.

•

Spread the batter into the prepared pan.

•

Mix together the remaining ^{1}/2 cup (100 grams) sugar and the
^{1}/4 cup (25 grams) cocoa powder and sprinkle evenly over
the top. Pour the hot coffee over the cake batter, then bake
for 25 minutes, until it appears just set around the edges yet
still slightly jiggly in the center.

Individual Hot Chocolate Cakes with White Chocolate Sauce

6 INDIVIDUAL CAKES

Small, warm chocolate cakes baked to order have become all the rage around the world for good reason. Who can resist a rich tower of chocolate with a moist, oozing center, served hot from the oven? I often double the chocolate impact with a dark chocolate sauce, such as the Tupelo Honey Chocolate Sauce with Brandy (page 133), served ladled over as a contrast to the white chocolate sauce.

> 10 ounces [285 grams] bittersweet or semisweet chocolate, chopped
>
> 4 tablespoons ($^1/_2$ stick) [60 grams] salted or unsalted butter
>
> 4 tablespoons [50 grams] sugar
>
> 4 large eggs, separated

White Chocolate Sauce

> $^1/_2$ cup [125 ml] heavy cream
>
> 5 ounces [140 grams] El Rey or best-quality white chocolate, chopped

Butter six 6-ounce (150-ml) custard cups or ramekins to use as cake molds. Sprinkle the insides with sugar and tap out any excess. Adjust the oven rack to the center of the oven and preheat to 400°F (205°C).

•

In a large heatproof bowl set over a saucepan of simmering water, melt the chocolate and butter together until smooth. Remove from the heat and whisk in 2 tablespoons (25 grams) of the sugar and the egg yolks.

•

In a clean, dry bowl, whip the egg whites with an electric mixer on medium speed, until they are frothy. Increase the speed and whip until the egg whites start to form soft, wet peaks. Whip in the remaining 2 tablespoons (25 grams) sugar and beat just until the whites form shiny, droopy peaks.

•

Fold one-third of the egg whites into the chocolate mixture to lighten it, then fold the remaining egg whites into the chocolate mixture.

•

Divide the batter into the prepared cake molds, set them on a baking sheet, and bake for 12 minutes, until they feel ever-so-slightly baked in the center. Remove from the oven and let stand for a moment before unmolding onto serving plates.

•

To make the sauce, bring the cream to a simmer, then remove from the heat and whisk in the white chocolate until smooth.

•

Surround the cakes with the white chocolate sauce.

Double Chocolate Soufflés

6 INDIVIDUAL SOUFFLÉS

I truly believe that I began my baking career the very same evening that my parents decided that I was old enough to stay home without a babysitter. It was the era of TV dinners, so I was occasionally left with a rock-hard frozen aluminum rectangle for dinner. One night, unsatisfied with the tiny square of dessert offered, I opened my mother's favorite cookbook, and lo and behold, I discovered a recipe for an exotic-sounding chocolate soufflé. All the ingredients were in the house, and with a Pyrex measuring cup as a soufflé dish, my career was born. Serve the soufflés immediately with a drizzle of crème anglaise or a dollop of whipped cream.

5 ounces [140 grams] bittersweet or semisweet chocolate, chopped

1/4 cup [60 ml] milk

6 tablespoons [70 grams], sugar

2 teaspoons whiskey, or 1 teaspoon vanilla extract

3 large egg yolks

4 large egg whites

1 1/2 ounces [45 grams] bittersweet or semisweet chocolate, very coarsely chopped, or 1/3 cup [45 grams] chocolate chips

Butter six 4-ounce (125-ml) ramekins or 6-ounce (150-ml) custard cups. Place them on a baking sheet. Preheat the oven to 400°F (205°C).

•

In a large heatproof bowl set over a pan of simmering water, melt the chocolate with the milk. Remove the pan from heat and whisk in 3 tablespoons (35 grams) of the sugar, the whiskey, and the egg yolks. Let stand at room temperature.

•

In a clean, dry bowl, whip the egg whites with an electric mixer on medium speed until they are foamy and begin to hold their shape when the whisk is lifted. Gradually whip in the remaining 3 tablespoons (35 grams) of sugar, whipping until the whites hold soft, droopy peaks.

•

Fold the beaten egg whites into the chocolate mixture. Fill the ramekins or custard cups halfway with the soufflé mixture. Sprinkle in the pieces of chopped chocolate. Add the remaining batter, filling the soufflé dishes almost to the top.

•

Bake for 14 minutes, or until the soufflés are firm, yet jiggly when nudged. They should be very soft when you remove them from the oven. Serve immediately.

•

Custard cups can be filled with the soufflé batter a few hours in advance and left at room temperature until ready to bake. Bake right before serving.

Caramelized Chocolate Almond Budino

ONE 9-INCH (23-CM) BUDINO, 12 TO 16 SERVINGS

This recipe is from my good friend Joanne Weir, who is a television host, cookbook author, travel guide, and cooking instructor. I've known Joanne a long time and I trust her taste, since she's cooked professionally for years. She raves about this recipe. I tried it and I was raving as well.

Amaretti cookies, which taste of bitter almonds, are available at well-stocked supermarkets and Italian grocers and give this dessert its indescribable aroma and flavor.

2 cups [400 grams plus 200 grams] sugar

2 cups (about 10 ounces) [285 grams] ground amaretti crumbs

1/2 cup [50 grams] finely ground almonds

3 tablespoons all-purpose flour

4 1/2 ounces [130 grams] bittersweet or semisweet chocolate, chopped

8 large eggs

3 cups [750 ml] whole milk

Have a 9-inch (23-cm) cake pan (not a springform pan) and oven mitts ready. In a large, heavy-duty sauté pan, melt 1 cup (200 grams) of the sugar over medium heat. As it heats, it will melt first at the edges. Very gently use a wooden spoon to stir the browned edges toward the center to encourage even browning. Cook, stirring as little as possible, until the sugar is deep golden brown. Remove from the heat. (If the sugar becomes grainy, remove it from the heat and stir it until the sugary crystals dissolve.)

●

Pour the caramelized sugar into the cake pan. Wearing oven mitts, immediately tilt the pan and swirl the hot caramel around to coat the bottom and the sides, being careful not to drip any hot caramel on yourself. Set aside. Preheat the oven to 375°F (190°C).

●

Mix the amaretti crumbs with the ground almonds and flour. In a large heatproof bowl, melt the chocolate over a pan of simmering water. Whisk in the remaining 1 cup (200 grams) of sugar, then the eggs one at a time, beating well after each addition. Finally, whisk in the milk to make a custard.

●

Whisk the amaretti mixture into the custard, then pour the batter into the caramelized sugar–coated cake pan. Set the pan in a larger pan (such as a roasting pan). Add warm water to the larger pan, so that the water reaches halfway up the outside of the cake pan, creating a water bath.

●

Bake for 65 to 75 minutes, until the cake feels set and relatively firm in the middle when gently pressed with a fingertip. Remove the budino from the water bath and let it cool at least 15 minutes, then invert it onto a serving plate. Cut the cake into wedges.

●

If the budino is not to be served within a few hours, it should be refrigerated. It can be refrigerated overnight.

Dark Milk Chocolate and Date Bread Pudding

10 SERVINGS

Adding silky nuggets of dark milk chocolate and sticky dates, accented with a whisper of spicy cinnamon and orange zest, is my personal victory combating the notion that bread pudding must always be unexciting and predictable. This bread pudding begs to be served warm from the oven. That way, all the chunky pieces of dark milk chocolate stay soft and melted. If baked in advance, rewarm the pudding in a low-temperature oven for about 10 minutes before serving. Dark milk chocolate has a higher percentage of cacao solids than ordinary milk chocolate. Excellent brands are Bonnat, El Rey, Guittard, and Omanhene (pages 33, 154, 51, and 68). Serve with whipped cream or chocolate sauce.

2 cups [500 ml] half-and-half

2 cups [500 ml] milk

Zest of 1 orange

$^1/_2$ teaspoon ground cinnamon

1 cup [200 grams] sugar, plus 1 tablespoon for sprinkling the top

4 large eggs

1 teaspoon vanilla extract

8 cups (about $^3/_4$ pound) [340 grams] firm-textured bread, cut into 1-inch (2.5-cm) cubes

$^3/_4$ cup [100 grams] snipped date pieces (pits removed), tossed in 1 tablespoon unsweetened cocoa powder to separate

10 ounces [285 grams] dark milk chocolate, chopped

Preheat the oven to 325°F (160°C). Butter a 9 x 13-inch (23 x 33-cm) baking dish.

•

In a large saucepan, warm the half-and-half, milk, orange zest, cinnamon, and the 1 cup (200 grams) of sugar.

•

Mix the eggs with the vanilla in a medium-sized bowl. Gradually stir the warm milk mixture into the eggs using a whisk to combine them.

•

Evenly distribute the pieces of bread in the baking dish and toss in the date pieces and milk chocolate chunks.

•

the great book of chocolate

Pour the custard over the bread and press down to soak the bread with the liquid. Sprinkle with the tablespoon sugar.

•

Bake for 45 minutes, then cool slightly.

•

Variation: Substitute 1 cup (240 grams) firmly packed light brown sugar for the granulated sugar in the recipe.

Fresh Mint and White Chocolate Crème Anglaise

ABOUT 2¹/₂ CUPS (625 ML)

Crème anglaise is a custard sauce cooked slowly on the stove top while stirring constantly. Master this rich, creamy sauce and you'll find it's a great accompaniment to just about any dessert, chocolate or otherwise. Try it with your favorite chocolate cake, or spoon the chilled custard over a bowl of berries in the summer.

2 cups [500 ml] whole milk
6 tablespoons [75 grams] sugar
¹/₂ cup [125 ml] packed crushed fresh mint leaves
4 ounces [115 grams] white chocolate, finely chopped
6 large egg yolks

In a medium saucepan, warm the milk with the sugar and mint leaves. Remove the saucepan from heat, cover, and steep for 30 minutes.

•

Meanwhile, prepare an ice bath using two bowls, one larger than the other, and have a strainer handy. Fill the larger bowl halfway with ice and water. In the smaller bowl (it should hold at least 2 quarts [2 liters]) add the chopped white chocolate.

•

Place the egg yolks in a medium bowl. Rewarm the milk, then gradually whisk it into the egg yolks. Pour the mixture back into the saucepan and cook over medium-low heat, stirring and scraping the bottom constantly with a heatproof spatula until the custard is thick enough to leave a trail when you draw your finger through it, about 3 to 5 minutes.

•

Strain the custard over the white chocolate and stir until the chocolate is melted. Cool the crème anglaise completely over the ice bath, stirring occasionally. Refrigerate until ready to serve.

White Chocolate Custard with Raspberries

4 SERVINGS

I serve these custards slightly warm, which softens the raspberries and releases their subtle, sweet perfume. Savor these with tiny, delicate silver spoons; something as dreamy and elegant as these quivering custards with their creamy-smooth white chocolate demands to be relished in small, measured doses.

1 1/2 cups [375 ml] half-and-half

4 ounces [115 grams] white chocolate, finely chopped

1/4 cup [50 grams] sugar

4 large egg yolks

2 teaspoons kirsch

1 1/2 cups [200 grams] fresh raspberries

In a small saucepan, warm the half-and-half with the white chocolate and sugar over low heat. Stir gently until the white chocolate is melted, then remove from the heat.

•

In a separate bowl, whisk the egg yolks. Gradually add the warm half-and-half mixture to them, stirring gently with the whisk. Add the kirsch.

•

Preheat the oven to 350°F (175°C).

•

Set four 4-ounce (125-ml) ramekins or 6-ounce (150-ml) custard cups in a baking pan with high sides. Add warm water to the larger pan, so that the water reaches halfway up the outside of the custard cups, creating a water bath. Cover the pan with foil and bake for about 40 minutes, or until the custards appear to be slightly jiggly when nudged.

•

Remove the custards from the water bath and cool on a wire rack.

•

Serve slightly warm, or at room temperature, topped with the fresh raspberries.

Chocolate Pudding

4 SERVINGS

Someone once asked me during an interview, "How do you prevent skin from forming on chocolate pudding?" When I replied, "The skin is the best part!" the host advised all listeners to send me their pudding skins. For the next few weeks I opened my mailbox with a certain amount of trepidation. (Just for the record, I only like *fresh* chocolate pudding skin.)

> 2 cups [500 ml] milk
> 4 ounces [115 grams] unsweetened chocolate, chopped
> 6 tablespoons [75 grams] sugar
> 1 tablespoon cornstarch
> 2 large egg yolks
> 2 teaspoons chocolate extract (see page 15), or 1/2 teaspoon vanilla extract
> 1 cup [250 ml] whipped cream
> 3 tablespoons shaved bittersweet chocolate

In a small saucepan, warm the milk and the chocolate until the chocolate is melted (it may not be completely smooth).

•

In a medium saucepan, make a slurry by whisking together the sugar, cornstarch, and egg yolks. Gradually whisk the warm milk and chocolate into the slurry.

•

Cook over moderate heat, stirring constantly with the whisk, until the pudding thickens , about 10 to 12 minutes. Remove from the heat and mix in the chocolate extract.

•

Divide the pudding among 4 custard cups and chill thoroughly before serving.

•

Garnish the puddings with a dollop of whipped cream and the shaved bittersweet chocolate.

•

If you do not want skin on top of your pudding, press a piece of plastic wrap over the top, forming a seal, before chilling.

Tupelo Honey Chocolate Sauce with Brandy

ABOUT 2 CUPS (500 ML)

Over the past few years, my friend Mäni Niall has acquired the title King of Honey. Going into his kitchen, he always seemed to be holding court over a panoply of honeys. The liquid kind, that is. Here's his suave recipe for dark chocolate sauce with the sexy secret of honey.

> 1 cup [250 ml] heavy cream
> 3 to 4 tablespoons Tupelo honey
> zest of 1 orange
> 4 ounces [115 grams] bittersweet or semisweet chocolate, chopped
> 1 ounce [30 grams] unsweetened chocolate, chopped
> 1 tablespoon brandy

Heat the cream and honey just until bubbles appear at the edges of the cream, but do not allow to boil.

•

Remove the mixture from the heat and add the orange zest. Let steep for 20 minutes. Reheat the mixture again just to the point that bubbles appear at the edge of the pan.

•

Place the chocolate in a medium bowl.

•

Pour the mixture through a fine-meshed strainer set over the chocolate. Discard the zest. Let the sauce sit a few minutes, then gently stir until smooth and creamy. Stir in the brandy.

•

Store at room temperature in an airtight container for up to 10 days.

Triple-Chocolate Parfait

ONE TALL 9-INCH (23-CM) CAKE, 8 TO 10 SERVINGS,
OR 8 GOBLETS

This recipe comes from Michael Lewis-Anderson, the
brilliant chocolate stylist from Wittamer in Brussels
(page 57), who swears he cannot make his parfaits fast
enough for chocolate lovers who come from all around
the world for his superlative creations.

When melting the chocolates, be sure that the bowls
are thoroughly dry first. Just a drop of liquid can cause
chocolate to become stiff and unmanageable. Since you
are making three distinct mousse layers, whip all the
cream in one bowl and then separate it into thirds, and
do the same with the egg whites. For a change of pace,
instead of serving the three mousses as a cake, divide the
recipe in half and layer the three mousses in 8 tall wine
goblets. They're especially elegant when topped with
shavings of dark, milk, and white chocolate, or perfect
berries during the summer.

> 9 ounces [255 grams] bittersweet or semisweet
>   chocolate, chopped
> 9 ounces [255 grams] white chocolate, chopped
> 9 ounces [255 grams] milk chocolate, chopped
> 2 1/4 cups [560 ml] heavy cream
> 9 large egg whites
> Chocolate shavings

Lightly oil a 9 x 3-inch (23 x 7.5-cm) springform pan and set it
on a serving platter.

•

In three separate medium-sized heatproof bowls, melt each
chocolate successively over a saucepan of simmering water
(you can use the same saucepan, just melt one after the
other). Remove each chocolate from the heat and set aside
to cool to lukewarm.

•

Whip the cream until it holds soft, droopy peaks. It should be
relatively stiff but not dry and curdled. You should have about
6 cups (1 1/2 liters) of whipped cream.

•

Making sure your chocolate is not hot, fold one-third of the
whipped cream (about 2 cups [500 ml]) into the dark chocolate in two separate additions.

•

(continued)

Divide the remaining whipped cream between the bowls of milk and white chocolate, then fold the cream into each.

•

In a clean bowl, beat the egg whites until they are thick and hold their shape, but not dry.

•

Fold one-third of the egg whites (about 2^1/$_2$ cups [625 ml]) into each chocolate mousse filling, folding until smooth.

•

Pour the dark chocolate mousse into the prepared cake pan and level the top. Add the milk chocolate mousse, spreading it over the dark chocolate mousse and leveling the top. (If the milk chocolate mousse seems thin, freeze the cake for about 30 minutes before adding the white chocolate mousse.)

•

Finally add the white chocolate mousse to the top. (It will seem thin, but that is fine.)

•

Chill the parfait cake for at least 6 hours, or freeze, before removing the sides of the cake pan. The cake should be sliced and served either chilled or frozen. Serve it with the chocolate shavings.

•

If you are concerned about serving uncooked egg whites, pasteurized egg whites are available in most grocery stores.

•

Variation: Replace the kirsch with 2 teaspoons Chartreuse liqueur added to the custard mix before baking.

the great book of chocolate

Chocolate Soufflé Tart with White Chocolate and Grand Marnier Cream

ONE 9-INCH (23-CM) TART, 8 TO 10 SERVINGS

This tart is heaped with a filling of the deepest, darkest, richest chocolate filling imaginable, then baked just until set. Chocolate desserts don't get any better than this.

9 ounces [255 grams] bittersweet or semisweet chocolate, chopped

8 tablespoons (1 stick) [115 grams] unsalted butter, cut into pieces

3 large eggs

1/4 cup [50 grams] sugar

One 9-inch (23-cm) prebaked tart shell

White Chocolate Grand Marnier Cream

2 ounces [60 grams] white chocolate, chopped

1 cup [250 ml] heavy cream, chilled

1 1/2 tablespoons Grand Marnier

Adjust the oven rack to the center of the oven and preheat to 375°F (190°C).

•

In a large heatproof bowl, melt the chocolate and the butter together over a saucepan of simmering water. Stir until smooth, then remove from the heat.

•

In the bowl of an electric mixer, beat the eggs and sugar until the mixture is foamy and thick enough to hold a shape when you lift out the beater, 5 to 10 minutes.

•

Fold the beaten eggs into the chocolate mixture until there are no streaks remaining. Scrape the filling into the baked tart shell and bake for 22 to 25 minutes, until the filling feels just set. Cool completely before serving.

•

To make the white chocolate cream, melt the white chocolate with 2 tablespoons of the cream and the Grand Marnier. Remove from the heat, stir until smooth, and let stand until room temperature.

•

Whip the remaining cream until it forms stiff peaks. Fold the white chocolate mixture into the cream in two additions, adding additional Grand Marnier to taste.

•

Serve the tart topped with a spoonful of the white chocolate cream.

Dark Milk Chocolate Ice Cream with Cacao Nibs

ONE QUART (1 LITER)

I devised with this recipe after tasting the crunchy and ultrachocolaty cacao nibs available from Scharffen Berger (page 19). Small, intensely flavored bits of roasted cacao beans, the nibs are usually conched into a paste to make chocolate. The nibs provide a great nut-like crunch with the added bonus of chocolate, providing a lively contrast to the creaminess of the dark milk chocolate ice cream.

> 8 ounces [225 grams] dark milk chocolate,
>   chopped
> 1¹/₂ cups [375 ml] heavy cream
> 1¹/₂ cups [375 ml] whole milk
> ³/₄ cup [150 grams] sugar
> Pinch of salt
> 4 large egg yolks
> 2 teaspoons cognac
> ³/₄ cup [90 grams] cacao nibs

Warm the milk chocolate and the heavy cream in a large heatproof bowl set over a pan of simmering water. Stir until the chocolate is melted, then remove from heat and set aside with a fine-meshed strainer nearby.

•

In a saucepan, warm the milk with the sugar and salt. Stir together the egg yolks, then gradually add some of the warm milk to them.

•

Pour the warmed eggs back into the saucepan and cook over low heat, stirring and scraping the bottom constantly with a heatproof spatula, just until the custard thickens enough to lightly coat the spatula, 3 to 5 minutes. Strain the custard into the milk chocolate mixture and stir together. Stir in the cognac. Chill thoroughly.

•

Place the mixture in your ice cream maker and freeze according to the manufacturer's instructions. Stir in the cacao nibs when you remove the ice cream from the freezing chamber.

Bourbon Mud Pie

ONE 9-INCH (23-CM) PIE, 8 TO 12 SERVINGS

This cool dessert is wonderfully refreshing due to a heady splash of bourbon added to both the ice cream filling and the topping. The great thing about making a mud pie is that it doesn't really require much cooking and can be assembled well in advance, using high-quality store-bought ice cream. When you're at the store, why not pick up a bunch of fresh, aromatic mint as well? I can't think of a better summer accompaniment than tall, iced mint juleps—the best way to use up any leftover bourbon. You may want to serve wedges of this pie with slightly sweetened whipped cream, flavored with bourbon or even peppermint extract, and a fresh mint leaf or two as a garnish.

Chocolate Crust

1 1/2 cups [150 grams] chocolate wafer cookie or chocolate graham cracker crumbs

3 tablespoons sugar

3 tablespoons butter (3/8 stick) [45 grams] unsalted butter, melted

Pie

4 to 5 cups [about 1.25 liters] (total) premium-quality coffee and chocolate ice creams

3 tablespoons bourbon

Glaze

5 ounces [140 grams] bittersweet or semisweet chocolate, chopped

2 tablespoons (1/4 stick) [30 grams] unsalted butter

1/4 cup [60 ml] bourbon

1/3 cup [50 grams] sliced almonds or chopped roasted peanuts

Preheat the oven to 375°F (190°C). Butter a 9-inch (23-cm) pie plate.

•

Toss the chocolate cookie crumbs with the sugar and butter until moist. Use your hands to press the crumbs evenly into the bottom of the pie plate and two-thirds of the way up the sides.

•

Bake the crust for 9 minutes. Remove from the oven and cool completely.

•

To fill the pie, chill a metal mixing bowl thoroughly. Quickly mash the ice cream in the bowl with the bourbon until it is spreadable. Smooth the ice cream into the piecrust and return the pie to the freezer.

•

When the pie is firm, make the glaze by melting together the chocolate, butter, and bourbon. Spread the glaze over the top of the frozen pie (it will firm up quickly) and return the pie to the freezer. Once frozen, cover the pie with plastic wrap until ready to serve.

•

To serve, garnish the pie with the toasted almonds or peanuts.

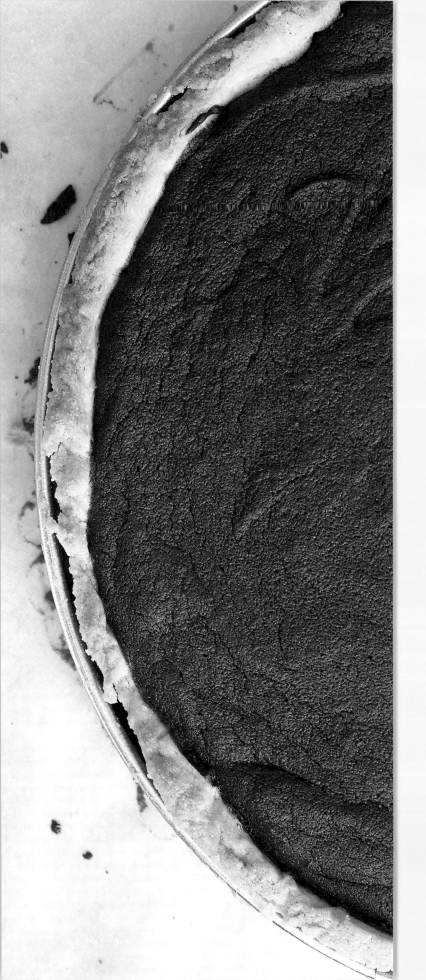

Chocolat Tarte de Rue Tatin

ONE 10^{1}/$_{2}$-INCH (27-CM) TART, 10 TO 12 SERVINGS

Being a pastry chef, I really don't know how to cook "regular" food. And believe me, you can't live on cake and cookies alone! I was lucky to spend time with Susan Herrmann Loomis in her home, where she teaches cooking, on *rue Tatin* in the French village of Louviers in Normandy. I spent an amazing week braising wild game, boning just-reeled-in fish, slicing farmhouse vegetables, and shaping rustic loaves of *levain* breads. As a reward, Susan assembled this incredibly intense chocolate tart for me, using the famous cream from Normandy as a treat for (I hope) a job well done.

- ^{1}/$_{3}$ cup [85 ml] heavy cream
- 16 ounces [450 grams] bittersweet chocolate (must be 52% to 55% cacao), finely chopped
- 4 large eggs, at room temperature
- One 10^{1}/$_{2}$-inch (27-cm) prebaked tart shell

Preheat the oven to 350°F (175°C).

•

In a medium-sized saucepan, heat the cream until it begins to bubble around the sides of the pan. Remove from the heat and stir in the chocolate, stirring until melted. Cool to room temperature.

•

Whisk the eggs one at a time into the chocolate mixture until smooth.

•

Spoon the filling into the prebaked tart shell and bake until the filling is set but not too firm, 15 to 20 minutes.

•

Remove the tart from the oven and cool to room temperature before serving.

•

Although you could serve this tart with something as simple as whipped cream, Susan served it with freshly churned cinnamon ice cream, which was sensational.

Homemade Rocky Road

A BIG BATCH, ENOUGH FOR 12 TO 16 PEOPLE

While living in France, I made this very American confection for startled Parisians, who had never heard of anything so strange in their lives. Peanuts and chocolate and marshmallows? All together?

The marshmallows can be made up to 1 week in advance, and stored in an airtight container. If you don't make your own marshmallows, you can substitute 4 cups (1 liter) of store-bought miniature ones.

Making Rocky Road is a fine way to practice tempering chocolate. See the expanded instructions and guidelines on pages 89–91, and follow my simple 3-step instructions below. Soon you'll be tempering like a pro.

1. Melt the chocolate to 120°F (49°C).
2. Cool the chocolate to the low 80°F (upper 20°C) range.
3. Carefully raise the temperature of the chocolate up to between 88°F and 91°F (31°C to 33°C), never higher.

Marshmallows

2 envelopes [14 grams] unflavored gelatin (powdered), such as Knox

$1/2$ cup plus $1/3$ cup [125 ml plus 85 ml] cold water

1 cup [200 grams] sugar

$1/3$ cup [85 ml] light corn syrup

4 large egg whites

Pinch of salt

2 teaspoons vanilla extract

$1 1/2$ cups [210 grams] cornstarch, plus more for dusting

$1 1/2$ cups [210 grams] powdered sugar

Rocky Road

$1 1/4$ pounds [565 grams] bittersweet or semisweet chocolate, chopped

$1 1/2$ cups [200 grams] roasted, unsalted peanuts (or another favorite nut, toasted)

$1/2$ cup roasted [60 grams] Scharffen Berger cacao nibs (optional)

In a small bowl, sprinkle the gelatin over the $1/2$ cup (125 ml) cold water to dissolve and soften. Set aside.

●

(continued)

In a small saucepan fitted with a candy thermometer, mix the sugar and corn syrup with the 1/3 cup (85 ml) of water. Place over medium-high heat.

•

In the bowl of an electric mixer, pour in the egg whites and beat on low speed until frothy. Add the pinch of salt.

•

When the syrup reaches between 210°F and 220°F (100°C and 104°C), increase the speed of the mixer and beat the egg whites until they are thick and fluffy (do not overbeat).

•

When the syrup reaches 245°F (118°C), as the mixer is whipping, slowly pour the syrup into the egg whites, pouring so that the syrup does not fall on the whisk (which can cause it to splatter and stick to the sides of the bowl). (You will use this saucepan again, to melt the gelatin, so don't wash it yet.)

•

Scrape the gelatin and water into the pan that you used for the syrup and swirl it to dissolve (it should be hot enough to dissolve the gelatin). Pour the liquefied gelatin into the egg whites as they are whipping. Add the vanilla and continue to whip for 5 minutes, or until the mixture is room temperature.

•

Mix the cornstarch and powdered sugar together. Using a sifter, dust an 11 x 17-inch (28 x 43-cm) (approximately) baking sheet evenly and completely with cornstarch. Use a spatula to spread the marshmallow mixture into a layer on the pan. Set the sheet aside to dry for at least 4 hours, or preferably overnight, uncovered.

•

Using a pizza cutter or scissors dusted with the powered sugar and cornstarch mixture, cut the marshmallows into any size or shape pieces. Toss the pieces in the sugar and cornstarch mixture. Working in batches, place the marshmallows in a wire strainer and shake vigorously until the excess sugar and cornstarch mixture falls away.

•

Cover a baking sheet with plastic wrap, parchment, or waxed paper.

•

Chop up all of the chocolate. Place 16 ounces (450 grams) of the chocolate in a heatproof bowl and melt it over simmering water, stirring frequently, until it is fully melted and smooth.

•

Remove the bowl from the simmering water and stir in the remaining 4 ounces (115 grams) of chocolate. Let stand, stirring occasionally, until the temperature falls to the low 80°F (upper 20°C) range.

•

"Flash" the bowl over the simmering water by putting it back over the water for 3 to 5 seconds at a time, stirring frequently, until the temperature reads between 88°F and 91°F (31°C and 33°C) (using care if using a breakable glass thermometer). You'll need to flash it several times to get it to the correct temperature. Don't be tempted to keep the chocolate over the heat until it reaches the proper temperature; it will continue to rise after you remove the bowl from the heat. (If the temperature rises over 91°F [33°C], you'll need to begin the process all over again.) Now your chocolate is tempered.

•

Immediately toss the marshmallows, peanuts, and cacao nibs into the tempered chocolate until just coated, stirring as little as possible because the chocolate cools as it is stirred and will set up quickly.

•

Heap the Rocky Road on the lined baking sheet, spread just a bit, and then chill until firm.

•

Cut the Rocky Road into irregular pieces and serve.

•

Store the candy at room temperature in an airtight container for up to 2 weeks (although you will not be able to keep it around for more than a day or so). Rocky Road makes great gifts, cut into hunks and tied securely in cellophane bags.

Chili con Chocolate

3 QUARTS (3 LITERS), ABOUT 8 SERVINGS

Most people only think of *mole* when using chocolate in a Mexican dish, but I have found that just a bit of chocolate stirred into a steaming pot of chili adds an authentic earthy quality. Traditionally, unsweetened (bitter) chocolate is used in savory dishes. But after experimenting with all sorts of fancy chocolate, I discovered true Mexican flavor comes in the disks of Ibarra, a very coarse, earthy Mexican chocolate studded with ground almonds, which, happily, is available at just about every Latin market in the world.

I like my chili rather spicy, and if you do too, use the full amount of cayenne that I suggest, along with the dried chiles. Pass bowls of shredded sharp Cheddar cheese or crumbled *queso fresco*, cooling sour cream, crispy sliced scallions, diced avocado, and chopped cilantro for guests to customize their own bowls.

1 1/2 cups [275 grams] dried pinto or kidney beans

6 cups [1.5 liters] water

2 tablespoons vegetable oil

2 medium onions, diced

1 green bell pepper, seeded and diced

4 cloves garlic, minced

1 jalapeño pepper, seeded and minced

1 tablespoon salt

2 pounds [1 kg] beef chuck, cut into 1/2-inch [1.3-cm] cubes, or 2 pounds [1 kg] ground beef or turkey

1 to 2 teaspoons cayenne

2 teaspoons dried oregano

1/2 teaspoon dried dill

1 teaspoon unsweetened cocoa powder, natural or Dutch-process

1 1/2 tablespoons ground cumin

Freshly ground black pepper

3 1-inch [2.5-cm] dried chile peppers (optional)

1 28-ounce [794 gram] can crushed tomatoes

3-ounce [85-gram] disk Ibarra Mexican sweet or bittersweet chocolate, chopped

2 teaspoons red wine vinegar

Rinse and sort the beans, discarding any stones. Place the beans in a medium saucepan and add the water. Bring the water to a boil, lower to a simmer, and cook for $1^1/_2$ hours, partially covered, until the beans are tender.

•

In a large stockpot, heat the oil. Add the onions, bell pepper, garlic, jalapeños, and salt, and cook for about 10 minutes over medium heat, until the onions and peppers soften. Add the beef, cayenne, oregano, dill, cocoa, cumin, black pepper, and dried chile peppers. Cook until the meat is cooked through.

•

Add the crushed tomatoes and the beans with their cooking liquid. Simmer the chili for at least 1 hour, uncovered, until thick. Stir in the chocolate and vinegar.

•

Chili is best made a day before serving to allow everything to thicken and meld nicely.

Chocolate Pizza Dough

ONE 11 X 17-INCH (28 X 43-CM) PAN PIZZA,
OR TWO 12-INCH (30-CM) ROUND PIZZAS

This is for the true (probably crazy) chocolate lover.
Chocolate adds an intriguing quality to pizza. Spicy toppings, like chorizo sausage and chiles, and dry, salty
cheeses make excellent additions. I like this best when
made with bittersweet or semisweet chocolate that has a
cacao content of at least 60%.

1 tablespoon active dry yeast

1 cup [250 ml] tepid water

1 cup plus 1^3/4 cups [135 grams plus 270 grams]
all-purpose flour

3 ounces [85 grams] bittersweet or semisweet
chocolate, chopped

2 tablespoons olive oil

1^1/4 teaspoons salt

A few turns freshly ground black pepper

^{1}/2 teaspoon cayenne pepper, or to taste (optional)

In the bowl of an electric mixer, or a large mixing bowl, sprinkle the yeast over the water. Stir in 1 cup (140 grams) of the flour and let stand 20 to 30 minutes.

•

Meanwhile, melt the chocolate with the olive oil. Set aside. Once the yeast mixture is foamy, add the melted chocolate, then gradually mix in the remaining 2 cups (280 grams) flour and the salt, pepper, and cayenne.

•

On a lightly floured countertop, knead the dough until smooth and elastic, about 5 minutes. Add 1 tablespoon of flour if the dough is too sticky and resists becoming smooth. Return the dough to the bowl, cover the bowl with a towel or plastic wrap, and let rise in a warm place for 1 1/2 hours, or until doubled in size.

•

Preheat the oven to 450°F (230°C).

•

Once risen, punch the dough down. To make a thick-crusted pan pizza, sprinkle a baking skeet with cornmeal. On a lightly floured surface, roll the dough into a rectangle to fit the baking pan. (Pizza dough is quite stretchy. To make it easy, roll the dough partially, let it rest a few minutes so the gluten will relax, and then continue. It will roll much easier.) Place the dough on the prepared baking sheet.

•

To make two round thin-crust pizzas, divide the dough in half, then roll each section into a 12-inch (30-cm) round. Place each round on a baking sheet dusted with cornmeal.

•

Cover the pizza with the toppings and cheese of your choice. For a pan pizza, let the dough rise for 20 minutes, then bake it. Thin-crust round pizzas are best baked immediately after the toppings are added. Bake the pizzas until the toppings bubble and the crusts are crispy.

Resources

Amedei
The costliest chocolate in the world, made in Tuscany from the rarest cacao beans on earth. www.amedei.com

The Association of the Chocolate, Biscuit and Confectionary Industries of the European Union
CAOBISCO takes an industry position regarding the addition of tropical fats to chocolate in the EU, a very controversial opinion among chocolate lovers. www.caobisco.com

Auguste Pralus
In Roanne, France, Auguste Pralus has been roasting his own cacao beans since 1955 and grinding them into chocolate for his confections. Ten different chocolates are available, including single-bean origin chocolates from Trinidad, São Tomé, and Ghana. Large bars available and also sample packs for comparing the various origins.
www.chocolats-pralus.com

Bad Candy
Lively and raucous discussions of crummy candies from around the globe. www.bad-candy.com

Barry-Callebaut
An alliance of French and Belgian chocolate producers, Barry-Callebaut supplies many professionals and home bakers with chocolate. Learn about how chips are made, or sign up for classes for professionals or amateurs at the Barry-Callebaut Institute. www.barry-callebaut.com

Bernachon
One of the world's great chocolate destinations, located in Lyon, France. Heavenly chocolates, all made from cacao beans roasted and blended in small batches just behind the magnificent chocolate shop and tea salon.
www.bernachon.com

Bernard Dufoux
French chocolatier Bernard Dufoux roasts and grinds cacao beans to make his own blends of chocolate. His tablets embedded with almond croquant or dried fruits are stunning.

At his shop in La Clayette, you can take a course in chocolate and arrange for a tour. www.chocolatsdufoux.com

The Biscuit, Cake, Chocolate and Confectionery Alliance of the United Kingdom

The alliance regularly monitors and reports on working conditions in cacao-producing regions, as well as on industry facts. www.bccca.org.uk

Blommer Chocolate Company

Popular U.S. chocolate maker. Look for their more upscale line of chocolates, simply called the Signature Line. www.blommer.com

Bonnat Chocolatier

A family-owned chocolate maker in Voiron, France. If you're coming to the region near the French alps, you can arrange to tour their production facility. www.bonnat-chocolatier.com

Cacao Sampaka

Barcelona's ultra-modern cacao experience, with beautiful, albeit palate-shocking, chocolates flavored with anchovies, tobacco, and truffles made with, gulp, real truffles. For the less-adventurous, sit at their chocolate tasting bar and nibble on chocolate-filled grilled sandwiches, or a slim tumbler of hot chocolate scented with jasmine or passion fruit. www.cacaosampaka.com

C'est Très Chic

Staggering collection, all for sale, of over 2,000 antique European and American chocolate molds in every theme imaginable. www.chocolatemold.net

Chocolate.com

Huge index of chocolate manufacturers around the world. Some assorted chocolates available for purchase as well. www.chocolate.com

Chocolate Man

Bill Richardson is a wondrous (and reasonable) source for a huge variety of chocolates, dipping tools, and a well-chosen selection of chocolate-making supplies. www.chocolateman.net

Chocolates El Rey

Makers of Venezuelan chocolate all from 100% criollo cacao. Superb dark, milk, and white "single-bean" chocolates. www.chocolates-elrey.com

Chocolate Snowball

Meet Letty Flatt, divine pastry chef and chocolatier. www.chocolatesnowball.com

The Chocolate Society

The Chocolate Society in the United Kingdom was founded in 1992 to enlighten and educate the public about all things chocolate. The society produces a newsletter, has a chocolate

shop in London, publishes a directory of chocolate shops.
www.chocolate.co.uk

Chocolove
Makers of organic Belgian chocolate bars.
www.chocolove.com

Chocophile
Reviews and ratings of chocolates, rumors and gossip about
the chocolate industry, and chocolate sample packs for sale
to formulate your own opinions. www.chocophile.com

Chocosphere
A virtual galaxy of chocolate, Chocosphere sells over 20
varieties of chocolate, many difficult to obtain. Grenada
Chocolate tablets, organic Swiss bars from Cocoa Camino,
and the beautifully designed chocolates by "the bald man"
from Israel, Max Brenner. www.chocosphere.com

Chocovic
This Catalan chocolate manufacturer makes only three
chocolates, one from each varietal of cacao: Ocumare,
Guaranda, and Guyave. All are excellent. Chocovic has a
school for professionals as well. www.chocovic.es

Chocovision
Makers of the Revolation chocolate tempering machines,
geared for home cooks. www.chocovision.com

Club des Croqueurs de Chocolat
This chic society meets in Paris to discuss and evaluate
chocolates. Membership is strictly limited to a privileged few,
but their website (which tends to move around) allows
everyone to see the results of their chocolate tastings, where
quality is rated by the number of chocolate bars. Check to
see who gets the coveted four-bar rating.
www.webenders.com/croqueurs/ or
www.croqueurschocolat.com

Dagoba
All organic chocolate bars, chocolate drops for baking, and
cocoa powder. Terrific flavored bars with unusual aromatics
such as lime, chai, and crunchy tropical nuts.
www.dagobachocolate.com

Dalloyau
Stunning French pastry and chocolate boutiques found
around Paris and Asia. www.dalloyau.fr

davidlebovitz.com
My website, which is updated regularly, with stories of
culinary adventures, recipes for chocolate desserts and more.
Learn about upcoming chocolate tours and classes that I lead
in Europe and across the United States.
www.davidlebovitz.com

Escribà

The most sumptuous chocolate shop in Barcelona. In the Spanish tradition, there's playful and elegant chocolate creations. Don't miss the towering chocolate sculptures in the back of the shop created exclusively for Spanish royalty and grand events. www.escriba.es

Fog City News

This San Francisco newsstand stocks well over 150 chocolate bars from just about everywhere, and has tasting notes from its staff. There's everything from chocolate bars flavored with strawberries and green peppercorns to chiles. www.fogcitynews.com

Fran's Chocolates

Fran Bigelow presents her superb cakes, truffles, and confections, available at her retail stores in Seattle or online. www.franschocolates.com

Green and Black's

Green and Black's in the United Kingdom uses organic cacao from Togo and Belize to make upscale, fine tablets of chocolates. www.greenandblacks.com

Guittard Chocolate

Learn about artisan E. Guittard's blends and single-bean varietal chocolates. www.guittard.com

Healthy Cocoa

England's Positive Food Company whips up a delicious cacao-based beverage, super-high in antioxidants. www.healthycocoa.com

Hershey's

Take the excellent virtual tour of the world's largest chocolate factory where 80 million Hershey's Kisses are made each day. www.hersheys.com

The International Cocoa Organization

You can learn about cacao beans and track the selling price of cacao on the world market at their website. The most comprehensive information about cacao available. I always lose track of time when visiting this site. www.icco.org

Jacques Torres

Pastry chef and owner of Jacques Torres Chocolates makes bonbons from his own chocolate, processed on site in New York City from roasted cacao beans. www.mrchocolate.com

La Maison du Chocolat

Perhaps the finest chocolate boutiques in the world. Simple and elegant, each chocolate is truly sublime. www.lamaisonduchocolat.com

Lenôtre

Aside from making some of Paris' greatest pastries and chocolates, Lenôtre operates an extraordinary school for professionals just outside of Paris, and a chocolate and baking school for home cooks off the Champs Elyées within Paris. www.lenotre.fr

Le Roux Chocolatier

This wonderful chocolatier makes unusual chocolates flavored with local ingredients from Brittany, including buckwheat and hops (which give the chocolates a haunting whisky flavor). Their unctuous C.B.S. caramels are truly the best in the world. C.B.S. stands for caramel-butter-salt. www.chocolatleroux.com

Madame Setsuko

Madame Setsuko chocolatier in Tokyo makes exquisite chocolates dusted with green tea as well as small truffles accented with colorful, seasonal flower petals. Unusually fine, delicate designs. www.setsuko.co.jp

Martine's Chocolates

Cream-filled chocolates voted #1 by Consumer Reports. www.martineschocolates.com

Mayordomo

Earthy, coarse, and traditional Mexican chocolate from Oaxaca made from cacao grown in Chiapas and Tabasco. www.mexichoco.com

The National Association of Cocoa Exporters of Ecuador

The NACEE is a union of Ecuadorian national exporters that also reports on working conditions, prices, and industry regulations. www.anecacao.com

National Confectioners Association

This happy (almost giddy) site is the home of the U.S.-based National Confectioners Association. Within are all sorts of fun reasons to eat more candy, along with recipes, jobs in the candy and chocolate industry, statistics, and the history of chocolate and candy production in the United States. www.candyusa.org

Nick Malgieri

Baking instructor, chocolate expert, and cookbook author extraordinaire. www.nickmalgieri.com

Nutella

Learn more about Nutella, the worldwide phenomenon combining chocolate and hazelnuts into a yummy spread. www.nutellausa.com

Omanhene

Dark milk chocolate made from cacao grown and manufactured in Ghana,Africa. www.omanhene.com

Padovani Chocolates

Honolulu chocolatier which incorporates flavors of the islands into his chocolates. www.padovanirestaurants.com

Pierre Marcolini
Contemporary and inventive Belgian pralines (the Belgian word for chocolates). Boutiques in Brussels and London. www.marcolini.be

Puyricard
Located in Aix-en-Province (with a shop in Paris as well), Puyricard enrobes *calissons* (almond-paste candies) with chocolate, and makes other assorted chocolates. The website has interesting information about chocolate history and production. www.puyricard.fr

Richard Donnelly Chocolates
Excellent chocolatier based in Santa Cruz, California. www.donnellychocolates.com

Recchiuti Confections
You'll find kits for making S'Mores, as well as slabs of intense brownies, fine chocolates delicately scented, and the most unctuous burnt caramels.
www.recchiutichocolates.com

Richart
Richart chocolates are distinctive for their crisp, clean lines and intriguing flavors, which change seasonally. Based in Lyon, France, there are Richart boutiques around the world. www.richart.com

Rococo
Chantal Coady's decidedly British chocolates from London, with flower essences, nougats, and marzipans. Organic chocolates as well. www.rococo.ro

Scharffen Berger Chocolate Maker
Handcrafted chocolate that jump-started the American artisan chocolate revolution. Blocks of chocolate for baking and snacking. Arrange for a factory tour in Berkeley, California. www.scharffenberger.com

Schokinag
A German manufacturer of high-quality chocolate for baking and confectionery. They've teamed up with Christopher Norman Chocolates in New York City to produce 1-pound bars for the serious (and hungry) home baker. www.schokinag.com

See's
See's is an American institution, making chocolates by hand with chocolate from Guittard, their Bay Area neighbor. The candy is very reasonably priced considering the quality. The snappy chocolate-covered molasses chips and almond toffee are classics. www.sees.com

Slitti
Avid chocolate-lovers describe Slitti chocolate as a religious experience. Extra-fine quality dark and high-percentage Italian milk chocolates, some with a whopping 70% cacao. www.slitti.it

Star Kay White

Makers of an intoxicating chocolate extract, which naturally heightens the flavor of anything baked with chocolate. Other extracts available. www.starkaywhite.com

Sweet Celebrations

Great source for candy making and baking supplies. Bulk chocolates, tempering machines, and candy packaging materials as well. www.sweetc.com

Sur La Table

Anything to do with baking can be found at Sur La Table. Chocolate molds, flavored oils, candy boxes, and cake pans of all sizes and shapes. Culinary classes at many locations. www.surlatable.com

Vanilla.com

Why vanilla in a chocolate book? Many chocolate manufacturers flavor their chocolates with aromatic vanilla beans and Patricia Rain's website is the best place to learn about the fascinating world of vanilla, cacao's tropical cousin. www.vanilla.com

Vosges Haut-Chocolat

There's always something sensual and intriguing at Vosges boutiques and tasting bars in Soho and Chicago. www.vosgeschocolate.com

Wittamer

The magical world of Wittmer chocolate from Brussels. If you visit, you'll be dazzled by the window displays, which change seasonally, featuring elaborate chocolate sculptures. www.wittamer.com

World Cocoa Foundation

Information about sustainable cacao harvesting, deforestation, worker's rights, and related issues. www.chocolateandcocoa.org

Yachana Gourmet

Unlike no other chocolate product on the market, made by caramelizing cacao nibs with cane or pineapple syrup. Yachana Jungle Chocolate is made in Ecuador, and its profits fund health centers. www.yachanagourmet.com

Zingerman's

This Midwest bakery and specialty shop carries a wide variety of chocolates. I love the Michel Cluizel sample packs, which allow you to taste and compare 8 different origins of cacao, conveniently contained in a single package. www.zingermans.com

Index